CW01033017

Richard Cannon

Historical Record of the Fifth Regiment of Foot, or Northumberland Fusiliers

Richard Cannon

Historical Record of the Fifth Regiment of Foot, or Northumberland Fusiliers

1st Edition | ISBN: 978-3-73406-297-1

Place of Publication: Frankfurt am Main, Germany

Year of Publication: 2019

Outlook Verlag GmbH, Germany.

Reproduction of the original.

PREFACE.

.

The character and credit of the British Army must chiefly depend upon the zeal and ardour, by which all who enter into its service are animated, and consequently it is of the highest importance that any measure calculated to excite the spirit of emulation, by which alone great and gallant actions are achieved, should be adopted.

Nothing can more fully tend to the accomplishment of this desirable object, than a full display of the noble deeds with which the Military History of our country abounds. To hold forth these bright examples, to the imitation of the youthful soldier, and thus to incite him to emulate the meritorious conduct of those who have preceded him in their honourable career, are among the motives that have given rise to the present publication.

The operations of the British Troops are, indeed, announced in the 'London Gazette,' from whence they are transferred into the public prints: the achievements of our armies are thus made known at the time of their occurrence, and receive the tribute of praise and admiration to which they are entitled. On extraordinary occasions, the Houses of Parliament have been in the habit of conferring on the Commanders, and the Officers and Troops acting under their orders, expressions of approbation and of thanks for their skill and bravery, and these testimonials, confirmed by the high honour of their Sovereign's Approbation, constitute the reward which the soldier most highly prizes.

It has not, however, until late years, been the practice (which appears to have long prevailed in some of the Continental armies) for British Regiments to keep regular records of their services and achievements. Hence some difficulty has been experienced in obtaining, particularly from the old Regiments, an authentic account of their origin and subsequent services.

This defect will now be remedied, in consequence of His Majesty having been pleased to command, that every Regiment shall in future keep a full and ample record of its services at home and abroad.

From the materials thus collected, the country will henceforth derive information as to the difficulties and privations which chequer the career of those who embrace the military profession. In Great Britain, where so large a number of persons are devoted to the active concerns of agriculture, manufactures, and commerce, and where these pursuits have, for so long a period, been undisturbed by the *presence of war*, which few other countries have escaped, comparatively little is known of the vicissitudes of active service, and of the casualties of climate, to which, even during peace, the British Troops are exposed in every part of the globe, with little or no interval of repose.

In their tranquil enjoyment of the blessings which the country derives from the industry and the enterprise of the agriculturist and the trader, its happy inhabitants may be supposed not often to reflect on the perilous duties of the soldier and the sailor,—on their sufferings,—and on the sacrifice of valuable life, by which so many national benefits are obtained and preserved.

The conduct of the British Troops, their valour, and endurance, have shone conspicuously under great and trying difficulties; and their character has been established in Continental warfare by the irresistible spirit with which they have effected debarkations in spite of the most formidable opposition, and by the gallantry and steadiness with which they have maintained their advantages against superior numbers.

In the official Reports made by the respective Commanders, ample justice has generally been done to the gallant exertions of the Corps employed; but the details of their services, and of acts of individual bravery, can only be fully given in the Annals of the various Regiments.

These Records are now preparing for publication, under His Majesty's special authority, by Mr. Richard Cannon, Principal Clerk of the Adjutant-General's Office; and while the perusal of them cannot fail to be useful and interesting to military men of every rank, it is considered that they will also afford entertainment and information to the general reader, particularly to those who may have served in the Army, or who have relatives in the Service.

There exists in the breasts of most of those who have served, or are serving, in the Army, an *Esprit du Corps*—an attachment to every thing belonging to their Regiment; to such persons a narrative of the services of their own Corps cannot fail to prove interesting. Authentic accounts of the actions of the great, —the valiant,—the loyal, have always been of paramount interest with a brave and civilized people. Great Britain has produced a race of heroes who, in moments of danger and terror, have stood, "firm as the rocks of their native shore;" and when half the World has been arrayed against them, they have fought the battles of their Country with unshaken fortitude. It is presumed that a record of achievements in war,—victories so complete and surprising, gained by our countrymen,—our brothers—our fellow-citizens in arms,—a record which revives the memory of the brave, and brings their gallant deeds before us, will certainly prove acceptable to the public.

Biographical memoirs of the Colonels and other distinguished Officers, will be introduced in the Records of their respective Regiments, and the Honorary Distinctions which have, from time to time, been conferred upon each Regiment, as testifying the value and importance of its services, will be faithfully set forth.

As a convenient mode of Publication, the Record of each Regiment will be printed in a distinct number, so that when the whole shall be completed, the Parts may be bound up in numerical succession.

FIFTH REGIMENT OF FOOT (NORTHUMBERLAND FUSILIERS).

[To face page 1.

HISTORICAL RECORD

OF THE

FIFTH REGIMENT OF FOOT,

OR

NORTHUMBERLAND FUSILIERS;

CONTAINING

AN ACCOUNT OF THE FORMATION OF THE REGIMENT
IN THE YEAR 1674,
AND OF ITS SUBSEQUENT SERVICES
TO 1837.

*PREPARED FOR PUBLICATION UNDER THE DIRECTION
OF THE ADJUTANT-GENERAL.*

LONDON:

PRINTED BY W. CLOWES AND SONS, 14, CHARING-CROSS.

MDCCCXXXVIII.

THE

FIFTH REGIMENT OF FOOT,

OR

NORTHUMBERLAND FUSILIERS,

BEARS ON ITS COLOURS

"ST. GEORGE AND THE DRAGON ,"

WITH THE MOTTO,

"QUO FATA VOCANT,"

AND THE FOLLOWING DISTINCTIONS:

*"Wilhelmsthal" —"Roleia" —"Vimiera" —"Corunna" —"Busaco"
—"Ciudad Rodrigo" —"Badajoz" —"Salamanca"—"Vittoria"
—"Nivelle" —"Orthes" —"Toulouse" —"Peninsula."*

FIFTH REGIMENT OF FOOT (NORTHUMBERLAND FUSILIERS).

HISTORICAL RECORD

OF THE

FIFTH REGIMENT OF FOOT,

OR

NORTHUMBERLAND FUSILIERS.

When the treaty of peace between England and Holland was being negotiated at London in February 1674,[1] the Dutch Government, remembering the advantages which had been derived from the Auxiliary British troops in former wars, obtained permission again to entertain in its service certain regiments.

Peace having been concluded, King Charles II. disbanded part of his army in the same year, when many of the officers and men proceeded to Holland, and the formation of the British division was commenced. The original design was to have a division of ten thousand men, to be commanded-in-chief, under the Prince of Orange, by Major-General Sir Walter Vane; but while the organization of this force was in progress, Sir Walter was killed at the battle of *Seneffe*, which was fought on the 11th of August, 1674; and Sir William Ballandyne was appointed to succeed him in the command of the British troops.

The formation making rapid progress, in the autumn, when the Prince of Orange was besieging *Grave* in North Brabant, he was informed that ten English and Irish companies, complete and fit for service, were at Bois-le-Duc, about 18 miles distant, and his Highness, eager to avail himself of their services, immediately ordered them to join the army. In this siege the ten companies gave presage of that gallantry for which they afterwards became celebrated; they lost several men, and Sir William Ballandyne was also killed by a cannon-ball.

The capture of *Grave*, which took place on the 28th of October, terminated the campaign; the troops were sent into quarters; and during the winter four regiments of British subjects were formed at Bois-le-Duc,—two English,—one Scots,—and one Irish;—the latter is now designated the FIFTH REGIMENT OF FOOT, OR NORTHUMBERLAND FUSILIERS, and its services form the subject of this narrative. Its first Colonel was Daniel O'Brien, Viscount of Clare; but this nobleman resigned soon afterwards, and quitted Holland. The regiment was commanded, *ad interim*, by Lieutenant-Colonel Anselmne, who had previously served with much honour in the Spanish service.

<u>1675</u>

In 1675 the command of this regiment was conferred on Colonel John Fenwick, who had distinguished himself at the battle of Seneffe; at this period the regiment discontinued the designation of "Irish," and many English gentlemen received commissions in it.

After leaving its quarters at Bois-le-Duc in the spring of 1675, the regiment was encamped for a short time on one of the beautiful plains of Louvain, and it was subsequently employed in manœuvring near the frontiers of France and in the Principality of Liege. The progress of the campaign was impeded by the severe indisposition of the Prince of Orange; no engagement of importance occurred, and in the autumn the regiment marched to the Dutch Netherlands and passed the winter in garrison at Utrecht.

<u>1676</u>

In the summer of 1676 the regiment marched to Brabant, and was stationed at Bois-le-Duc, preparatory to some expedition of importance. This occurred in the early part of July, and the men were in high spirits, anticipating some splendid adventure. About two o'clock in the morning the drums beat "to arms;" the regiment immediately assembled at the alarm-post, and commenced its march for the province of Limburg, being joined by other corps every day. On the fifth day, the Prince of Orange appeared at the head of the troops, and, to the surprise of the enemy, the famous city of *Maestricht* was besieged. This city, which was well fortified with all the works which art could suggest, was defended by 8000 chosen men commanded by Monsieur Calvo, a resolute Catalonian. The Prince of Orange attended to the progress of the siege; and after the arrival of the battering train, the works were carried on with vigour.

The three English regiments[2] were formed in one Brigade, and they soon distinguished themselves, beating back the sallies of the garrison with great slaughter. On the 30th of July, a storming party of two hundred men, furnished in equal proportions by the three regiments, attacked the Dauphin Bastion, and after a severe contest effected a lodgment, but afterwards lost their ground: this proved a sanguinary affair, and 150 men were killed and wounded out of the two hundred. On the 2nd of August the Brigade was again on duty in the trenches, when Colonel Fenwick was wounded.

The Prince of Orange resolved to make a second attack on the Dauphin Bastion on the 4th of August, when a detachment from the Brigade, commanded by Captain Anthony Barnwell of Fenwick's regiment, with another from the Dutch Foot Guards, commanded by Baron Sparr, formed the storming party.[3] At three o'clock the Brigade was under arms with the storming party in front; and at five the gallant little band, advancing under a tempest of bullets, went cheering to the attack and carried the bastion in gallant style—the English, gaining the lead of the Dutch, first made a lodgment. Scarcely, however, had the soldiers gained a footing, when the French sprung a mine and blew many of the men into the air, and following this up with a fierce attack, regained possession of the works. The heroic English were, however, "resolute to win;"—they returned to the attack, and fighting with a strength and majesty which nothing could withstand, drove back the French, and re-established themselves on the bastion; but their commander, Captain Barnwell, was killed, and more than half the officers and men of the party were killed and wounded.

About five in the morning of the 6th of August a desperate sally was made by three hundred Swiss Infantry, and, owing to the neglect of a sentry, they surprised and made prisoners the English guard on the bastion; but a reinforcement from the Brigade came forward to their rescue, and, after saluting the assailants with a few volleys, and a shower of hand-grenades, made a furious charge, retaking the bastion and chasing the Swiss Infantry with prodigious slaughter to the palisadoes of the counterscarp, destroying the whole detachment, except about twenty men who escaped into the town. The Prince of Orange complimented the Brigade on its distinguished bravery, and made each of the three regiments a present of a fat ox and six sheep.[4]

On the 15th of August Colonel Fenwick's regiment, commanded by Lieutenant-Colonel Wisely (the Colonel not having recovered from his wounds) was on duty in the trenches, when the enemy made another furious sally; but they were nobly received by the regiment; a fierce combat ensued, in which the strength and unconquerable spirit, of the English again excited the admiration of the Prince of Orange, and a reinforcement arriving, the French were driven back with great loss.

The progress of the siege had been marked by surprising energy, but it was prolonged by the resolute defence of the garrison; and when all things were ready for a general assault, a French army of overwhelming numbers, commanded by Marshal Schomberg, advanced to its relief. The Prince of Orange immediately raised the siege and retired; and the three English regiments, having sustained a severe loss, and having nearly half the number of the surviving officers and men wounded, were sent into quarters of refreshment in Holland. At the same time a misunderstanding occurred between Colonel (afterwards Sir John) Fenwick and the Prince, and the Colonel resigned his commission; when his Highness gave the Colonelcy of the regiment to the Lieutenant-Colonel, Henry Wisely.

The French, while amusing the Allies with negotiations for a peace, commenced the campaign of 1677, with great vigour, and with such an immense army, that the feeble preparations of the Dutch, and the apathy of the Spaniards, left the Prince of Orange without an army capable of resisting the enemy. He, however, resolved to attempt the relief of St. Omers, which was besieged by the French; the English Brigade was ordered to West Flanders, to take part in the enterprise, and it was encamped a short time on the plains of the Yperlee. In the early part of April, the Prince advanced with his little army, and on the 11th of that month he fought the battle of *Mont-Cassel* under great disadvantages in numbers, and in the nature of the ground. The English Brigade behaved with its usual gallantry; but the army was defeated, and the Prince retreated with the loss of his baggage and artillery. The Brigade was afterwards employed in manœuvring and in defensive operations until the autumn, when it went into quarters. The Prince of Orange proceeded to England, and was married to the Princess Mary on the 14th of November, 1677.

Before the following spring, Major-General the Earl of Ossory arrived from England to command the six British regiments in the Dutch service, and ten thousand English troops, commanded by the Duke of Monmouth, were ordered to proceed to Flanders to take part in the war.

The Earl of Ossory's brigade was early in the field: it was employed a short time on detached services in the Netherlands, and was afterwards encamped near the ground where the battle of Waterloo was fought in June, 1815. In the mean time the French besieged *Mons*, the capital of the province of Hainault, and their covering army occupied a strong position, with its right at the Abbey of *St. Denis*, and its left at Mamoy St. Pierre. The Prince of Orange assembled his army, and after advancing several stages, he encamped near the little river Senne, about seven miles from Mons; and on the morning of the 14th of August, 1678, his Highness put the troops in motion to attack the enemy.

The British Brigade, led by the Earl of Ossory, moved from its camp along a difficult tract of country, until it came in front of a hill occupied by the enemy's left wing, where it was destined to make its attack, in conjunction with the Dutch Foot Guards. The signal for the attack was given, when the British Grenadiers, springing forward with lighted matches, threw a shower of hand-grenades, which, bursting amongst the ranks of the enemy, did much execution. The Musqueteers followed, and opening a sharp fire, were answered by the volleys of the enemy; their fire was soon succeeded by the charge of the Pikemen, who went cheering onward to the attack, while the Musqueteers, drawing their swords, joined in the onset with admirable spirit and resolution,—and the enemy gave way. One attack was succeeded by another; the French, driven from field to field, still rallied and returned to the fight. Pike to pike and sword to sword, the combatants maintained a fierce conflict, while the hand-grenades flew in every direction, and the heights of Castehau presented a varied scene of turmoil and slaughter, in the midst of which the Prince of Orange and the Duke of Monmouth appeared, mixed with the combatants, and urging forward the storm of battle.[5] A French captain levelled his pistol at the Prince, but General D'Auverquerque killed the captain before he had time to fire, and thus saved his Highness's life, for which service the States made him a present of a valuable sword. Night at length put an end to the fight, and the French afterwards made a precipitate retreat.

The regiment lost in this action Lieutenant-Colonel Archer, Lieutenant Charlton, and about fifty men killed: also Major Hales, Captain Charlton, Captain Coleman, Captain Floyd, Captain Dupuy, Lieutenant Augerne, Lieutenant Marchany, Lieutenant Wilson, Ensign Barnwell, Ensign Arnesby, and upwards of a hundred men wounded. The loss in the other regiments of the Brigade was also equally great.

In the mean time preliminary articles for a treaty of peace had been agreed upon at Nimeguen; a cessation of hostilities took place on the day after the battle; and the Brigade, after encamping a few months in Flanders, marched to Holland, where it received the thanks of the States-General for its meritorious services.

The restoration of peace was followed by a reduction in the numbers of the Dutch Army; but the Prince of Orange, and the States-General of the United Provinces, were so sensible of the advantages they had derived from the services of the British troops, that they were desirous of retaining the six regiments in their service. A new treaty was concluded on this subject, and the States agreed to send the regiments to England, whenever the King required them to do so.

| 1679 |
| 1680 |

Colonel Wisely's regiment was marched to Grave, where it was employed on garrison duty four years; and in 1680, its Colonel having been drowned when on his passage to England, the Colonelcy was conferred on Lieutenant-Colonel Thomas Monk, of Sir Henry Bellasis' regiment (now Sixth Foot).

| 1684 |

Upon the prospect of hostilities with France, in 1684, the regiment marched from Grave, and was encamped for a short time near Brussels, and afterwards on the banks of the Dender; but no war breaking out, it proceeded into quarters at Mechlin.

1685

In the succeeding year the death of King Charles II. and the accession of James II., a professed Papist, being followed by a rebellion in Scotland, headed by the Earl of Argyle, and another in England, headed by the Duke of Monmouth, the six British regiments were applied for by the King, and they were accordingly embarked for England under the command of the following officers:—

Three English Regiments. { Colonel Thomas Monk,—now Fifth Foot.
Colonel Sir Henry Bellasis,—now Sixth Foot.
Colonel Alexander Cannon,—afterwards disbanded.

Three Scots Regiments. { Colonel Kirkpatrick.
Colonel Sir Alexander Colyear.
Colonel Hugh Mackay.

The three Scots regiments were, in the first instance, ordered for Scotland, but the rebellion in the North having been suppressed, they landed at Gravesend on the 30th of June, 1685, and having been reviewed on Blackheath by the King, marched through London towards the West.[6] The three English regiments landed a few days afterwards; but the rebel army having been defeated at Sedgemoor, on the 6th of July, they encamped on Blackheath, and afterwards on Hounslow Heath, where the Brigade was assembled and reviewed by his Majesty, and the efficiency, discipline, and appearance of the several corps, excited universal admiration.[7] The rebellion having been suppressed, the six regiments returned to Holland, and were again employed in garrison duty. The three English regiments were on the English establishment from the 5th of June, to the 3rd of August, 1685, and the Scots' regiments a few days longer.

1686
1687

The arbitrary proceedings of King James, with his advances towards the subversion of the Protestant religion, occasioned much anxiety to the Prince of Orange, who was married to the presumptive heiress to the throne; at the same time, the King was jealous of the attachment of the nation to his son-in-law, and in 1687 his Majesty demanded the return of the British regiments in the Dutch service. The States-General, in concert with the Prince, resolved not to part with these favourite corps, for whose services they expected soon to have urgent occasion; at the same time they laid no constraint upon the officers, but allowed them either to remain in Holland or to return to England, at their own free choice. Out of two hundred and forty officers,[8] only sixty[9] embraced the latter alternative; the rest bound themselves "to stand by and defend the Prince of Orange against all persons whatsoever."

| 1688 |
| 1689 |

The colonelcy of the regiment having become vacant by the death of Colonel Monk, it was conferred by the Prince of Orange on Lieutenant-Colonel Thomas Tollemache,[10] formerly of the Coldstream Guards.

The violent proceedings of the British Court at length occasioned many of the nobility to solicit the Prince of Orange to come with an armed force to their aid; and as the fate of all the other Protestant States in Europe appeared to depend on the preservation of Great Britain from Papal domination, the Prince and the States-General acquiesced. Thus the six British regiments had the honourable and glorious privilege of engaging in an enterprise for the deliverance of their native land from the attempts to establish Popish ascendancy, and the consequent chances of civil war. On receiving positive advice of the preparations in Holland, "the King was speechless, and, as it were, thunderstruck. The airy castle of a dispensing arbitrary power raised by the magic spells of jesuitical councils vanished away in a moment, and the deluded monarch, freed from his inchantment by the approach of the Prince of Orange, found himself on the brink of a precipice, whilst all his flatterers stood amazed and confounded."[11] The King at length assembled an army of about 30,000 men, and sent Lord Dartmouth to sea with the fleet.

FIFTH REGIMENT OF FOOT (NORTHUMBERLAND FUSILIERS) 1688.

The Prince of Orange's army, consisting of about 15,000 men, of which "the most formidable were the six British regiments,"[12] put to sea, after some delay from tempestuous weather, on the 1st of November, 1688; "the trumpets sounding, the hautboys playing, the soldiers and seamen shouting, and a crowd of spectators on the shore breathing forth their wishes after them."[13] Sailing in three divisions, the first, consisting of the English and Scots, commanded by Major-General Mackay, under a red flag; the second, being the Prince's Guards and the Brandenburgers, commanded by Count Solms, under a white flag; and the Dutch with a corps of French Protestants, commanded by the Count of Nassau, under a blue flag: they passed

17

triumphantly through the British Channel and landed on the Devonshire coast on the 5th of November. Colonel Tollemache's regiment (the Fifth) landed at Brixham key, two miles from Dartmouth, from whence it marched to Exeter and afterwards to Honiton, where, on the night of the 13th, it was joined by a number of men of the Earl of Oxford's and Duke of St. Alban's regiments of horse, and of the Royal Regiment of Dragoons, who had quitted the service of King James to espouse the national cause. These desertions were followed by others of a more important character; and King James, discovering that his army would not be subservient to his designs against the kingdom, fled to France, William and Mary, Prince and Princess of Orange, were solicited to ascend the throne; and thus the Revolution was happily effected without that sacrifice of human life which such events usually occasion. Colonel Tollemache's regiment had, in the mean time, marched to the vicinity of London, and it afterwards proceeded into quarters in the western counties. It was now permanently placed on the English establishment, and taking date from the 5th of June, 1685, the day on which it first received pay from the British crown, as before stated, it obtained rank as Fifth Regiment of Foot in the British Line.

Colonel Tollemache having been promoted to the command of the Coldstream Guards, the Colonelcy of the Fifth was conferred on Lieutenant-Colonel Edward Lloyd, by commission dated the 1st of May, 1689; and in the following month the regiment marched from the west of England for London, and was quartered in Southwark until October, when it embarked at Deptford and Greenwich for Plymouth, and in December marched into Cornwall, with detached companies in Devonshire.

| 1690 |

In the mean time Ireland had become the seat of war, and King James was at the head of the Roman Catholics, and a French auxiliary force, in that kingdom, while the Duke of Schomberg commanded the Irish Protestants and English troops; and in the spring of 1690 the Fifth Foot was ordered thither. The regiment, accordingly, proceeded to Bristol, where it embarked; and having landed at Belfast on the 20th of April, marched to Lisburn, and encamped near the banks of the Lagan until the 9th June, when it proceeded to Armagh and erected its tents on the undulating grounds in that neighbourhood, where an encampment was formed of four regiments of English infantry, with three regiments of Danish horse and eight of foot.

King William having arrived in Ireland, the regiment marched to Dundalk, where the army was assembled; and on the 1st of July the enemy was attacked in his position on the banks of the river *Boyne*. The Fifth was in Brigadier-General Trelawny's brigade, and by its gallant conduct it contributed to the signal victory gained on this occasion. The enemy evacuated Dublin a few days after the battle, when the regiment was ordered to proceed thither, and it remained in garrison in that city during the remainder of the campaign.

| 1691 |

The regiment left Dublin in the early part of 1691, and in April it was stationed at Mountmelick. The troops quartered in that neighbourhood were frequently disturbed by bands of armed Roman Catholic peasantry, called *Rapparees*, who concealed themselves in the day-time, and at night prowled about the country, committing every description of depredation: to check these proceedings, a detachment of 200 men of the F$_{IFTH}$, commanded by Major Rider, with 100 men of Lord George Hamilton's regiment, and 50 troopers of Colonel Byerley's Horse,—now 6th Dragoon Guards,—the whole commanded by Major Wood,[14] marched out of Mountmelick at nine o'clock on the evening of the 4th of May, and, dividing themselves into several small parties, they traversed the woods and bogs for several miles, frequently encountering lurking parties of the enemy, whom they attacked, killing seventy men and capturing a quantity of cattle, which Major Wood sent to Mountmelick under a guard of thirty men. The remainder continued their search until about ten o'clock on the following day, when Major Wood, with one party of 34 horsemen, and 30 foot, discovered two battalions of the enemy's regular army of about 400 men each, marching silently between the wood and mountains, not far from *Castle-Cuff*; at the same time the enemy espied Major Wood and his little detachment. The English, with a noble bearing and audacity, formed up in a ploughed field to oppose this formidable host, and the Irish instantly sent forward their grenadiers to commence the attack, but perceiving the undaunted countenance of the detachment, they halted at a distance. A sharp firing was at this instant heard beyond the forest, and Major Wood, apprehending that the party with the cattle was attacked, proceeded to its assistance; but Lieutenant Ellis and the thirty foot, behaved like valiant men; and, having repulsed a superior force, effected their retreat with the booty. The firing had brought a detachment of 80 men of the F$_{IFTH}$ from the opposite side of the forest, and Major Wood, having now 34 horsemen and 110 foot with him, resolved, notwithstanding the disparity of numbers, to attack the enemy's column. He accordingly divided his foot into two parties, and directed them to attack the enemy in front, while he himself with the horse made a short compass to gain the enemy's rear. This gallant little band, advancing boldly against the enemy's masses, commenced the attack with a fury and resolution which the Irish could not withstand, and they attempted to retreat; but at that moment Major Wood with his thirty-four troopers came galloping from amongst the trees and charged the flank of the column with admirable courage and resolution; the heavy horse, breaking through the ranks, trampled down the Irish in a terrible manner. The column was now become a confused rabble, scattered in wild disorder, and cut down by the English horsemen on every side; while the English foot, slinging their muskets and drawing their swords, joined in the pursuit and chased the enemy a considerable distance. One hundred and fifty of the Irish were killed on the spot; and 1 major, 5 captains, 9 lieutenants, 2 ensigns, 1 adjutant, 1 surgeon, 6 serjeants, 17 corporals, 3 drummers, and 82 private men, were made prisoners; 150 muskets were also collected, which the Irish had thrown away to facilitate their flight. "And all this was done by 110 of our foot and 34 horse. With the foot were Major Rider, Captain Nenny, Captain Dixey, Lieutenant Barton, and Ensign Russel. With the horse, were Cornet Jocelyn, Cornet Hasleton, and Adjutant Robinson, with Quarter-masters Davies and Cadford; who all, both horse and foot, behaved extremely well, and with the loss only of one corporal killed, and Adjutant Robinson, with two foot soldiers and one trooper, wounded[15]."

On the 12th of May, another party of the regiment was out scouring the woods, when 18 Rapparees were killed and several made prisoners.

In June, the FIFTH advanced with the army to *Athlone*, and took part in the siege, which was commenced on the 19th of that month: on the 30th the Grenadier company formed part of the storming party commanded by Major-General Mackay. The attack was made at six in the evening, when the forlorn hope, consisting of Captain Sandys, with 2 Lieutenants and 60 Grenadiers, all in armour, entered the Shannon, which was breast high, under a sharp fire, and were followed by the remainder of the storming party, who passed, some at the bridge of boats, and others by planks laid across the broken arches of the stone bridge. The party, having gained the opposite shore, threw forward a shower of hand-grenades, which put the Irish in confusion; then gallantly ascending the breaches forced their way through every obstacle, and in less than half an hour were masters of the town, with the loss of only 12 men killed, and 5 officers with 30 men wounded; but the enemy had about 500 men killed. Colonel Lloyd was appointed Governor of Athlone, and when the army advanced, the FIFTH, and Lieutenant-General Douglas's regiments, were left in garrison; and the battering train was left in their charge.

After the battle of Aghrim, when the army was about to besiege *Limerick*, the FIFTH, and a party of Militia, were ordered to advance with the heavy artillery; they, accordingly, left Athlone on the 12th of August, and joined the army at Cariganless on the 16th. The siege was commenced a few days afterwards, and the FIFTH was actively employed until the surrender of the place on the 3rd of October. This conquest terminated the war in Ireland, and the regiment, being immediately ordered to embark for England, landed at

Highlake, near Chester, on the 29th of December, from whence it marched to Nottingham, Derby, and other inland towns, where it commenced recruiting its numbers.

Three weeks, however, only elapsed before it was ordered to march to London, where it remained but a few days, and towards the end of February 1692 embarked for Flanders to join the army of the Allies, who were engaged in a war with France. The regiment was scarcely placed in cantonments in West Flanders, when the King of France assembled about 20,000 men near La Hogue, and ordered his fleet to prepare to convey them to England, with the view of replacing King James on the throne; the Second, F$_{IFTH}$, and Fourteenth regiments of Foot were consequently ordered to return: and these corps, having landed at Greenwich in the early part of May, were stationed along the southern coast. In the mean time the British and Dutch fleets had put to sea, and while England and France were gazing, in anxious expectation, at these preparations, the French fleet sustained a decisive defeat off La Hogue, and the alarm of invasion vanished. The F$_{IFTH}$ continued in extensive cantonments near the coast until October, when it marched to Portsmouth to perform duty in that garrison.

During the summer of 1693 the regiment was embarked on board the fleet, and, proceeding with an expedition to *Martinico*, it effected a landing, drove the enemy's troops from the coast, and laid waste several French settlements on that Island. In the autumn it landed at Portsmouth and marched into cantonments in Berkshire and Buckinghamshire.

The severe loss sustained this summer by the Allies at the battle of Landen, occasioned a strong reinforcement to be sent to Flanders during the winter, and the F$_{IFTH}$ was one of the regiments selected for foreign service. It accordingly embarked at Greenwich and Deptford in December, and, after landing at Ostend, marched to Sluys, a fortified town situated on an arm of the sea, where the regiment remained several months.

After leaving Sluys in the middle of May, 1694, the regiment pitched its tents on the levels near Ghent, and afterwards at Tirlemont in South Brabant, forming part of the army commanded by King William III. in person. On the 15th of June it was detached, with other corps, to take post near the Abbey of Lenthen. During the subsequent part of the campaign it was employed in several military operations, and in the autumn marched into barracks at Bruges. The death of its Colonel having taken place on the 26th of August, his Majesty conferred the vacant Colonelcy on Lieutenant-Colonel Thomas Fairfax, by commission dated the 6th of November, 1694.

After remaining in garrison at Bruges until the 25th of May, 1695, the FIFTH took the field and was encamped a short time on the verdant plains near the river Lys; and when King William undertook the siege of the strong fortress of *Namur*, the regiment formed part of the covering army commanded by the Prince of Vaudemont.

While the King was carrying on the siege, a French force of superior numbers, commanded by Marshal Villeroy, advanced to attack the covering army. On the evening of the 14th of July the Allies were formed in order of battle; the immense columns of the enemy were seen in the open grounds in their front, and the hostile armies passed the night under arms, expecting to engage at the break of day; at the same time the French had detached a division under Monsieur de Montal to turn the right flank of the allied army. This occasioned the Prince to order a retreat, which he masked with excellent judgment: the cavalry advancing to the front, the dragoons dismounting and forming on foot; while the artillery, and infantry with their pikes trailed, quietly withdrew. The enemy, anticipating success, prepared for the attack; but in a moment, the British dragoons, retiring a few paces, mounted their horses, and when the enemy thought to have commenced the battle, the skeleton squadrons withdrew; presenting to the surprised French the magic spectacle of what appeared to be an army vanishing out of sight. The enemy's cavalry galloped forward in pursuit; but the Allies continued their retreat in good order, and at six o'clock on the morning of the 16th were in position in front of Ghent.

The FIFTH was afterwards engaged in a series of manœuvres for the preservation of the maritime towns of Flanders, and for the protection of the troops before Namur. In the early part of August it was encamped between Genappe and Waterloo, and subsequently before Namur, which capitulated on the 22nd of August. From Namur the regiment marched to Nieuport, and encamped on the sand-hills near that town; and, remaining in the field until late in the season, when the weather was particularly wet and cold, the men were ordered to build straw huts; but towards the end of October they marched to Bruges.

On the 12th of May, 1696, the regiment marched out of the barracks at Bruges, and encamped behind the banks of the canal near the town. During the campaign of this year its services were limited to the protection of Ghent and Bruges from an attack which the French commanders made several demonstrations of a design of making on these towns; and it passed the winter in its former station at Bruges.

| 1697 |

From Bruges, the regiment marched, in the spring of 1697, to Brussels; and on the 12th of April proceeded through the forest of Soigne and pitched its tents near the village of Waterloo, where an encampment was formed of twelve regiments of infantry under the Count de Noyelles. The FIFTH was subsequently employed in a series of defensive operations until September, when the war was terminated by the treaty of Ryswick; and, being ordered to return to England immediately afterwards, it landed in December,—eight companies at Greenwich and two at Dover.

| 1698 |

The regiment remained but a short time in England before it was ordered to proceed to Chester, where it embarked for Ireland, and in August, 1698, it arrived at Dublin.

| 1704 |

On the 5th of February, 1704, Queen Anne appointed Colonel Thomas Pearce from a newly-raised regiment of foot (afterwards disbanded) to the Colonelcy of the FIFTH in succession to Thomas Fairfax.

| 1706 |
| 1707 |

During the early part of the war of the Spanish succession, this regiment was stationed in Ireland; but the united English, Dutch, and Portuguese armies having, in 1706, advanced to Madrid, the enemy cut off their communication with Portugal; the troops retired from Madrid to Valencia and Catalonia, and from that period their only communication with Portugal was by sea. At the same time it was found necessary to have a small army on the frontiers of Portugal, and the FIFTH, Twentieth, Thirty-ninth, and a newly-raised regiment commanded by Colonel Stanwix, having been selected for this service, sailed from Cork on the 22nd of May, 1707, and landed at the capital of Portugal on the 8th of June[16]. This seasonable reinforcement arriving soon after the defeat of the allied army at Almanza, in the south-east of Spain, and at the moment when the enemy, having captured Serpa and Moura in the Alentejo, had seized on the bridge of Olivenza in Portuguese Estremadura, and menaced that important place with a siege, its presence revived the drooping spirits of the Portuguese. The four regiments, being the only British troops in that part of the country, were disembarked with every possible expedition, and marched to the frontiers under the command of the Marquis de Montandre, when the enemy immediately ceased to act on the offensive and retired[17]. The four regiments, having halted at Estremos, a strong town of the Alentejo, situate on an agreeable tract on the Tarra, remained in this pleasant quarter during the summer heats, and afterwards encamped in the fruitful valley of the Caya near Elvas, having detached parties on the flanks to prevent the enemy making incursions into Portugal, in which service the regiments were engaged until November, when they went into quarters in the towns on the frontiers of Portugal.

1708

The regiment again took the field in the spring of 1708, and was encamped at Fuente de Sapatores between Elvas and Campo Mayor. The British division was soon afterwards increased to six regiments, by the arrival of the Thirteenth[18] and a newly-raised regiment (Paston's) from England; and the little army in the Alentejo was commanded by the Marquis de Fronteira; but the characteristic inactivity of the Portuguese occasioned the services of the FIFTH to be limited to defensive operations. It was encamped in the autumn at Campo Mayor, and afterwards proceeded into cantonments.

1709

After moving from its quarters in the spring of 1709, the regiment was again engaged in active operations. It was first encamped near Estremos, from whence it proceeded on the 23rd of April to Elvas, and was subsequently encamped with the army on the banks of the Caya, where the Earl of Galway, who had been removed from the army in Catalonia, appeared at the head of the British division.

On the 7th of May the French and Spaniards, commanded by the Marquis de Bay, marched in the direction of Campo Mayor, when the Portuguese generals, contrary to the advice of the Earl of Galway, resolved to pass the *Caya* and attack the enemy. The Portuguese cavalry and artillery took the lead, and, having passed the river and gained the opposite heights, opened a sharp cannonade; but upon the advance of their adversaries to charge, these squadrons faced about and galloped out of the field, leaving their cannon behind. The British division, arriving at the moment, repulsed the enemy; and the leading brigade, consisting of the Thirteenth, Stanwix's, and Galway's regiments, commanded by Brigadier-General Thomas Pearce, charging with great fury, recaptured the Portuguese guns; but the three regiments, pressing forward too far, were surrounded and made prisoners, and with them Major-Generals Sankey and the Earl of Barrymore, and Brigadier-General Thomas Pearce, fell into the hands of the enemy[19]. At the same time the FIFTH, Twentieth, Thirty-ninth, and Lord Paston's regiments, though deserted by the whole of the cavalry, made a determined stand, bearing the brunt of the enemy's reiterated attacks with admirable firmness, until the Portuguese infantry had retired; then moving to the rear in firm array—while the balls flew thick on every side, and the Earl of Galway's horse was shot under him, —the enemy coming on in full career, threatening the destruction of this little band; yet, with ranks unbroken and steady tread, these undaunted English calmly retraced their steps—exhibiting one of the most noble spectacles of war,—and occasionally punishing the temerity of their pursuers with a cool and deliberate resolution which laid a thousand Spaniards dead upon the field[20], and impressed the enemy, and also the Portuguese, with a sense of British courage and magnanimity. Thus they effected their retreat, with the loss of only one hundred and fifty men killed and wounded, and passed that night at Arronches.

The FIFTH acquired great honour by its signal gallantry on this occasion. It was afterwards encamped at Elvas, was subsequently in position on the banks of the Guadiana, and again passed the winter in cantonments in the Alentejo.

1710

The casualties of the preceding campaign having been replaced by recruits from England, the FIFTH again took the field in the spring of 1710, and was employed in the Alentejo; but the army was weak and unequal to any important undertaking, and the French having had some success in the province of Tras os Montes, occasioned a detachment to be sent thither. In the autumn the army advanced across the Guadiana, and on the 4th of October arrived at the rich plains of *Xeres de los Cabaleros* on the river Ardilla in Spanish Estremadura. It was resolved to attack this place by storm on the following day, and the FIFTH, Twentieth, and Thirty-ninth, British regiments, having been selected to perform this service under the command of Brigadier-General Stanwix[21], advanced at four in the afternoon to attack the works near St. Catherine's gate by escalade: a few minutes after the regiments had commenced the assault, the governor sent proposals to surrender, which were agreed to, and the garrison, consisting of 700 men, were made prisoners of war. The army afterwards retired to Portugal by the mountains of Orlor, and went into quarters. This summer the army on the other side of Spain gained two victories, and advanced to Madrid, when the most pressing instances were made by King Charles III. and General Stanhope, to induce the army of Portugal to advance upon the Spanish capital; but the Portuguese generals were unwilling to engage in so great an undertaking.

1711

During the campaign of 1711, the F<small>IFTH</small> formed part of the army which assembled at Olivenza in May, and, having passed the Guadiana by a pontoon bridge at Jerumencha, advanced against the enemy, who took refuge under the cannon of Badajoz. The F<small>IFTH</small> was afterwards engaged in the capture of several small towns, and in levying contributions in Spanish Estremadura; but the summer passed without any occurrence of importance, excepting a discovery made by the Earl of Portmore, who commanded the British troops in Portugal, of a clandestine treaty in progress between the crown of Portugal and the enemy, in which the former had agreed to separate from the Allies; and, to give an excuse for this, a mock battle was to have been fought, in which the British troops were to have been sacrificed[22]. This treaty was broken off, but the British Government soon afterwards entered into negotiations with France.

1712

The F<small>IFTH</small> continued in Portugal, and was encamped during the summer of 1712 on the pleasant plains of the Tarra. In the autumn a suspension of hostilities was proclaimed at the camp by Major-General Pearce, and the regiment went into cantonments.

1713

From Portugal, the regiment proceeded to Gibraltar, which fortress had been captured by an English and Dutch force in 1704, and was ceded to Great Britain in 1713 by the treaty of Utrecht, when the Earl of Portmore was appointed Governor; and the protection of the place was confided to the F<small>IFTH</small>, Thirteenth, and Twentieth regiments. Here the regiment remained in garrison for a period of fifteen years; its establishment was 500 men, and it became as celebrated for its excellent conduct in time of peace, as it had been distinguished for its noble bearing and gallantry in war.

1726

The crown of Spain had relinquished its claim on Gibraltar with reluctance, and having, towards the end of 1726, resolved to engage in a war with Great Britain, a Spanish army was assembled in Andalusia under the command of the Count de la Torres, to commence hostilities with the siege of this desirable entrepôt to the Mediterranean. This gave the F<small>IFTH</small> another opportunity of signalizing itself, and of adding to its honours already acquired,—the proud distinction of a successful defence of this important conquest.

1727

The preparations of the enemy were made upon a most extensive scale. Their troops were encamped before the place in January, 1727, the bringing up of cannon, mortars, and stores to the camp, occupied several weeks, and the heavy artillery was removed from the works at Cadiz and other fortified towns; at the same time the whole disposable force, including part of the garrison of almost every town in Spain, was assembled to take part in the siege. The works having been commenced in February, before any declaration of war was made, and persisted in against the remonstrance of the Lieutenant-Governor, Colonel Jasper Clayton, a council of war of the commanding officers of regiments was assembled, and a determined opposition was resolved upon. On the 21st of February the garrison opened its fire on the besiegers, and from that day the storm of war raged round the rocks of Gibraltar with dreadful violence, increasing in fury until the roar of a hundred cannon and the fire of small arms became almost incessant in the day-time, and was partially continued throughout the night, with the most fatal effects to the Spaniards, whose loss was particularly great. This contest was continued with a few partial intermissions until many thousands of the besiegers had perished in the attempt; while the tremendous fire of the Spaniards had produced little effect beyond the bursting of many of their own cannon, and the enlarging of the touchholes of others so as to render them useless. In the early part of June the fire slackened, and on the 18th of that month hostilities ceased. Thus the ostentatious vaunts of Spain terminated in defeat and confusion.

| 1728 |

The Fifth embarked from Gibraltar on the 12th of April, 1728, and proceeded to Ireland, in which country it remained seven years.

| 1732 |

In September 1732, General Thomas Pearce, who had commanded the regiment for twenty-eight years, was removed to the Fifth Horse, now Fourth Dragoon Guards, and was succeeded by Colonel John (afterwards Sir John) Cope from the Thirty-ninth regiment.

| 1735 |
| 1737 |

The regiment left Ireland in 1735, and was stationed in England in that and the following year; but in 1737 it again proceeded to Ireland. At the same time Colonel Cope was removed to the Ninth Dragoons, and the Colonelcy of the Fifth was conferred on Alexander Irwin.

| 1738 |

A period of seventeen years was now passed by the regiment in Ireland, where it continued to retain its high state of discipline and efficiency, and preserved untarnished the laurels it had previously won.

After the decease of Colonel Irwin, in 1752, the command of the regiment was given to Charles Whiteford; who was succeeded on the 20th of August, 1754, by Lord George Bentinck.

In the spring of 1755, the regiment left Ireland, and was quartered in England; and in September of that year it had the honour to receive King George II. at Chelmsford, on his way from Harwich to London.

The regiment remained in the south of England during the two succeeding years; and in 1758, another war having broken out, it formed part of an expedition designed to effect the reduction of the maritime power of France, and to make a diversion in favour of the Hanoverians. It accordingly proceeded to the Isle of Wight,—the general rendezvous,—embarked at Cowes eight hundred and eighty-eight men strong on the 25th of May, and its grenadier company was the first to make good its landing on the coast of France on the evening of the 5th of June, when seven companies of French foot, and three troops of dragoons, were quickly dispersed. On the 7th the army advanced in two columns;—the F_{IFTH}, taking the main road to *St. Maloes*, encamped in the evening about a mile from the town, and after sunset furnished, in common with the other regiments, a detachment, which, proceeding to the harbour, set fire to the shipping, magazines, &c., when a grand yet dreadful scene of conflagration presented itself. Having destroyed a valuable fleet and all the stores, the troops re-embarked and returned to England.

In August of the same year, the F_{IFTH} was engaged in a second expedition to the coast of France, when *Cherbourg* was captured, and the harbour, forts, magazines, and ordnance, consisting of 173 pieces of iron cannon and 3 mortars, were destroyed: at the same time 22 pieces of fine brass cannon, and two brass mortars, were brought off as trophies, and sent to England; and these guns, having been seen by King George II. in Hyde Park on the 16th of September, were conducted in procession through the city to the Tower of London.

The F_{IFTH} was also engaged in the descent made on the coast of Brittany on the 4th of September, when the batteries in the bay of St. Lunaire were destroyed, and the troops, marching into the interior, crossed the Drouette and Equernon, and advanced to Matignon, while the fleet proceeded to the Bay of St. Cas; thus alarming the country with the view of producing the return of the

28

French army from Germany. While the F$_{IFTH}$ was in France, some sharp skirmishing occurred, and when the troops re-embarked at St. Cas, the enemy attacked the rear-guard and occasioned considerable loss. The loss of the F$_{IFTH}$ in these three descents was ninety-five men. Towards the end of September the regiment landed at Cowes, and, having encamped a short period near Newport, went into quarters.

1759

The decease of Lord George Bentinck having occurred in 1759, Studholme Hodgson was appointed to the Colonelcy of the F$_{IFTH}$, from the 50th regiment.

1760

In the mean time the war was continued in Hanover and the neighbouring States, and the F$_{IFTH}$, having been ordered to proceed to Germany, embarked at Gravesend on the 12th of May, 1760, and arrived in the Weser on the 22nd of that month. After landing near Bremen, the regiment marched up the country, and joined the allied army commanded by Ferdinand Duke of Brunswick, at Fritzlar in Hesse-Cassel, on the 17th of June; when the grenadier company was detached to form, with the grenadier companies of the other regiments, two Battalions, which, being united in Brigade with the Scots Highlanders, usually formed the advance-guard of the army.

The regiment, after being employed in several manœuvres, formed part of the corps commanded by the hereditary Prince of Brunswick, which marched on the 10th of July to take post on the heights of *Corbach*; but found the ground occupied by the enemy in force; when a sharp skirmish occurred in which the F$_{IFTH}$ lost five men.[23]

Towards the end of July the regiment was encamped at Kalle. At 11 o'clock on the night of the 30th of that month it marched with the main army for Liebenau, and, having crossed the Dymel, advanced at five on the following morning to attack the enemy in his position on the heights of *Warbourg*.

The German corps and British grenadiers in advance having commenced the action, the French retired before the English infantry arrived. "No troops could show more eagerness than they showed. Many of the men, from the heat of the weather, and overstraining themselves to get on through morasses and difficult ground, suddenly dropped down on their march.[24]" The grenadier company of the F$_{IFTH}$, being in the column which commenced the attack, highly distinguished itself[25], and had four men killed, and Captain Ross, Lieutenant Baker, and twenty-six men, wounded.

The regiment remained for some time encamped near Warbourg; and the grenadier company, being encamped on the heights of Wilda, was engaged, on the night of the 5th of September, in surprising a French force in the town of *Zierenberg*, which service was performed with distinguished gallantry and success. The grenadiers were afterwards detached to the Lower Rhine, and were engaged in the attempt to surprise the enemy's camp at Rheinberg on the morning of the 16th of October, when a sharp action was fought at the Convent of *Campen*, in which the company of the F<small>IFTH</small> lost several men. In December the regiment left the camp at Warbourg, and went into cantonments in the villages on the bank of the Weser.

| 1761 |

In February, 1761, it again advanced, and, having crossed the Dymel, proceeded through a deep snow into Hesse-Cassel, where it had great success in several actions with the enemy; but returned to its former quarters in March.

The regiment again took the field in June, forming part of the Marquis of Granby's corps, and, after some manœuvring and skirmishing, it was encamped upon the heights in front of *Kirch-Denkern* in the bishopric of Paderborn. This post was attacked on the 15th of July, and was defended by the British troops with admirable firmness and resolution, and eventually the enemy was driven back with great loss. The attack was renewed by the enemy on the following morning with great fury, when the F<small>IFTH</small> displayed its usual spirit and determination in the defence of its post; and, after five hours' sharp fighting, some disorder appearing in the enemy's ranks, the regiment advanced to the charge and routed the enemy; at the same time the grenadier battalion, of which the company of the F<small>IFTH</small> formed a part, took prisoners the regiment of Rouge (formerly Belsunce) with its cannon and colours. The F<small>IFTH</small> lost in this action, Lieutenant Lillewood, 2 serjeants, and 9 men killed; also two officers, 5 serjeants, and 12 men wounded.

The regiment remained at its post near Kirch-Denkern until the 27th of July; it was afterwards employed in manœuvring and skirmishing in various parts of the bishopric of Paderborn and on the river Weser, and in September, it was employed in a diversion in the country of Hesse. It was engaged, on the 5th of November, in forcing the enemy's post at *Capelnhagen*, and on the 6th and 7th it took part in slight skirmishes at *Eimbeck* in the Electorate of Hanover. The grenadier company of the F<small>IFTH</small> was also engaged in a skirmish at *Foorwohle* on the 7th of November, and again on the 10th of that month, when the combatants were knee deep in snow. On the 12th the regiment encamped on the banks of the Huve near Eimbeck, from whence it proceeded in the early part of December into cantonments in the bishopric of Osnaburg.

| 1762 |

Having passed the winter amongst the rude peasantry of Osnaburg, the regiment again took the field, and joined the camp on the heights near Blumberg on the 4th of June 1762, from whence it proceeded to Corbeke.

The enemy took post at *Groebenstien*, and Prince Ferdinand formed a design of surprising them in their camp. For this purpose the army was formed into several columns. The FIFTH forming part of the centre column, left its camp before daylight on the morning of the 24th of June, and crossed the Dymel at Liebenau at four o'clock; then, advancing a distance of nine miles through a rugged and woody country, arrived in front of the enemy's camp, and commenced a sharp fire. The French, surprised and confounded, abandoned their camp, leaving their tents standing, and commenced their retreat: at the same time General Stainville threw himself with his division into the woods of *Wilhelmsthal* to favour the movement. Against this division, the right column of the allies, commanded by the Marquis of Granby, and the centre column under Prince Ferdinand, immediately advanced.

The FIFTH, commanded by Lieutenant-Colonel Thomas Marlay, taking the lead of the centre column, threw itself into the wood, and opened its fire with good effect; at the same time the Marquis of Granby's column attacked the enemy's rear. The French made a spirited resistance; but the FIFTH pressed forward with a conquering violence which overcame all opposition, while the main body followed in full career, and the Marquis of Granby intercepting the enemy's retreat captured many prisoners; when the remainder of the French division (excepting two battalions that escaped) after one fire, surrendered to the FIFTH[26]. After the French had surrendered, an officer of the FIFTH regiment, who went up to receive their colours from their standard-bearer, was shot dead upon the spot by a French serjeant who was standing near. This circumstance might have led to much bloodshed, but, fortunately, little confusion resulted; the serjeant was instantly put to death, and the colours were quietly taken possession of[27]. The loss of the regiment was Lieutenant Robinson, killed; and 1 serjeant, and 11 men wounded; also six men taken prisoners in the skirmish at the commencement of the action. Its conduct on this occasion excited much admiration;—as a mark of distinction the men were permitted to exchange their hats for the French grenadier caps; and the regiment for many years afterwards, wore a fusilier's cap instead of the hat then used by the infantry of the line. In commemoration of the gallantry displayed by the FIFTH Regiment on this occasion, his Majesty King William IV. was graciously pleased, in 1836, to authorize the regiment to bear the word 'WILHELMSTHAL' on its Colours and Appointments.

After the action the FIFTH encamped on the heights of Wilhelmsthal; it was subsequently employed in several operations; and on the 23rd of July, the grenadier company was engaged in a gallant affair at *Lutterberg*, when the Saxons under Prince Xavier were driven from their post and thirteen pieces of ordnance were captured. On the 24th of the same month one hundred men of the regiment were engaged with other corps in dislodging a detachment of the enemy from the heights of *Homburg*. The regiment was subsequently employed in operations on the Ohm, and the Lahn, and in several skirmishes in which it lost many men. It also formed part of the covering army during the siege of *Cassel*, which was terminated by the surrender of the place on the 1st of November. Shortly afterwards a suspension of hostilities took place; which was followed by a treaty of peace, concluded at Fontainbleau, and the regiment was ordered to return to England.

1763

It accordingly marched from Germany, through Holland, to Williamstadt, where it embarked on the 22nd of February, 1763[28], and landed in England in the early part of the following month. In May of the same year it proceeded to Bristol and embarked for Ireland, where it arrived on the 2nd of June, and landed at Passage near Waterford.

1764

The regiment passed the next ten years in Ireland, and was so remarkable for its cleanliness and attention to dress and appointments, that the men were usually called "The Shiners."

1767

Early in the year 1767 a system of honorary distinctions for long-continued good behaviour was introduced into this regiment, which was found to stimulate the indifferent to good conduct, and those already worthy, to perseverance in well-doing, and it produced such a body of non-commissioned officers as few corps could boast of. These distinctions consisted of three classes of medals[29] to be worn, suspended by a ribbon, at a button-hole of the left lappel; the first, or lowest class, which was bestowed on such as had served irreproachably for seven years, was of gilt metal, bearing on one side the badge of the regiment, *St. George and the Dragon*[30], with the motto "*Quo fata vocant*;" and on the reverse, "Vth Foot, MERIT." The second was of silver, bearing on one side the badge and motto, and on the other, "Reward of fourteen years' military merit." The third was similar to the second, but was inscribed with the name of the individual whose conduct had earned it: "A. B., for twenty-one years' good and faithful service as a soldier, had received from his commanding officers this honourable testimony of his merit." These medals were bestowed only upon soldiers who, for the respective periods of seven, fourteen, or twenty-one years, had never incurred the censure of a court-martial: they were given by the commanding officer at the head of the assembled battalion; and if, which rarely happened, the owner of a medal subsequently forfeited his pretensions to enrolment among the men of merit, his medal was cut from his breast by the drum-major as publicly as he had been invested with it. Those who obtained the third, or twenty-one years' medal, had also an oval badge of the colour of the facings on the right breast, embroidered round with gold and silver wreaths, and inscribed in the centre with the word "M$_{ERIT}$" in letters of gold.

1768

On the 7th of November, 1768, Lieutenant-General Hodgson was succeeded in the Colonelcy of the F$_{IFTH}$ by Hugh, Earl Percy, afterwards Duke of Northumberland. Earl Percy, when Colonel, duly estimating the good effects produced by this Regimental "Order of Merit," kept it up with all the liberality and dignity it deserved; and the following order, issued by him on the subject, is referred to in Adye's Essay on Rewards and Punishments, viz.: "Earl Percy having perceived, with great pleasure, the happy effects of the regimental Medals of Merit, influencing the non-commissioned officers and soldiers of the F$_{IFTH}$ to deserve the favour of their officers, and being anxious, as far as may be in his power, to encourage them to persevere in such sentiments of honour, is determined, for the future, to give them out every year, a short time before the review, instead of the usual day, as it often has happened that the regiment has been separated, which prevented the men, who were entitled to that mark of honour, from receiving it in so public a manner as his Lordship could wish."

1771
1772

During the stay of the F$_{IFTH}$ in Ireland it was frequently engaged in the service of the revenue; and also in suppressing the outrageous proceedings of bands of armed peasantry called Whiteboys, Hearts of Steel, and Hearts of Oak, and particularly against the latter in 1772, at and near Guildford in the north, where the house of Richard Johnson, Esquire, was attacked and reduced to ashes, and a clergyman, the Rev. Mr. Meroll, was barbarously murdered by these misguided insurgents.

1774

The regiment remained in Ireland until the unfortunate misunderstanding between Great Britain and her North American Colonies assumed an aspect so formidable, that it was deemed necessary to send additional forces to that country. The F$_{IFTH}$ was one of the corps selected to proceed on this service; and, having embarked at Monkstown near Cork on the 7th of May, 1774, it landed in the beginning of July at Boston, the capital of the state of

Massachusetts, which had recently been the scene of violence and outrage, particularly of the destruction of an immense consignment of Tea by the provincials. After landing, the regiment was encamped near the town for some time; a body of troops was assembled at this place under the Governor of the province, General Gage, and several fortifications were constructed.

| 1775 |

During the winter a determination to proceed to open resistance became general in the American States; they embodied a militia force, and in April 1775, a circumstance occurred which occasioned the display of these hostile designs. The occasion was the collection of some military stores at *Concord*, in Middlesex county, about eighteen miles from Boston; when General Gage sent the grenadiers and light infantry, including the companies of the FIFTH, under the orders of Colonel Smith, to destroy those stores. This detachment embarked in boats on the evening of the 18th of April, and, having proceeded a short distance up Charles river, landed on the marshes of Cambridge and proceeded to the village of *Lexington*, where it arrived at day-break and found a company of the militia formed up near the entrance of the town. These men were ordered to lay down their arms, but they did not comply; some desultory firing immediately occurred, which was followed by a volley from the troops which laid ten of the militia dead upon the spot, wounded several others, and dispersed the remainder: thus was the first blood drawn in this unhappy contest. After this skirmish, the troops continued their march to Concord, detaching six Light Infantry companies to take possession of the bridges beyond the town, while the remainder of the detachment effected the destruction of the military stores. In the mean time the country had been alarmed by the firing of guns and the ringing of bells: and a division of provincial militia was seen advancing towards the bridges, but they avoided committing any hostile act until the light infantry companies had killed two men, when the Americans instantly opened a sharp fire, and by their superior numbers forced the King's troops to retire. The country now appeared swarming with armed men, who fired on the troops on all sides, while numbers followed in their rear, and during the six miles' march from Concord to Lexington, skirmish succeeded skirmish, and a continued but irregular fire was sustained until the detachment had expended nearly all its ammunition. Fortunately it was met at Lexington by Earl Percy (Colonel of the FIFTH), who had been sent forward to support the detachment with his brigade and two pieces of artillery, and his lordship after a short halt made dispositions for continuing the march to Boston[31]. But the moment the troops were in motion the attacks became more frequent and more violent than before, the Americans hovering in hundreds upon the rear and keeping up a sharp fire from houses, from behind walls, trees, and other coverts, on both sides of the road; yet the troops, displaying a steady and noble bearing, united with a high state of discipline and undaunted spirit, marched under all these difficulties, in perfect order, a distance of fifteen miles to Charlestown, where they arrived at sunset, quite exhausted from a march of about thirty-five miles, on a hot day, and experiencing the extraordinary fatigues already mentioned. From Charlestown the troops crossed the river by the ferry to Boston, under cover of the fire of the men-of-war. The loss of the FIFTH, in this day's skirmishes, was five men killed; with Lieutenant Thomas Baker, Lieutenant William Cox, Lieutenant Thomas Hawkshaw, and fifteen men wounded; also one man taken prisoner[32].

This affair was followed by the appearance of the whole province in arms; —an immense number of men invested Boston, where the King's troops were stationed, on the land side; and on the morning of the 17th of June, it was ascertained that they had constructed works on *Bunker's Hill*—a high ground beyond the river. A body of troops, of which the FIFTH formed a part, was ordered to attack the heights; and this force, having embarked about noon, landed without opposition and formed up on some high ground near the shore. The enemy appearing resolved to defend this post, the ships of war opened their fire upon the works, while the King's troops, advancing under cover of the guns, went boldly to the attack; and commenced one of the most sanguinary actions on record. The FIFTH, ever emulous of glory, was seen ascending the hill on the side next Charlestown with signal intrepidity, and bravely sustaining its ancient reputation. Captain Harris (afterwards the conqueror of the Mysore) while leading on the grenadier company, was severely wounded, and obliged to quit the field, but he had in Lieutenant Lord Rawdon (afterwards Marquis of Hastings) a successor in command, who emulated and equalled the intrepidity of his disabled captain. Eventually the troops were staggered by the resolute tenacity of the defence, and the superior numbers of the enemy; yet, recovering, they appeared in a moment fired by a new ardour, and with fixed bayonets they went cheering forward with determined bravery and resolution,—encountering the Americans in close combat and driving them, after a sharp contest, out of the works. The King's troops were now established on *Bunker's Hill*, which they afterwards fortified and occupied in force. The loss of the FIFTH was 22 men killed; Captain Harris, Captain Jackson, Captain Downes, Captain Marsden, Lieutenant M'Clintock, Lieutenant Croker, Ensign Charleton, Ensign Ballaguire, 10 Serjeants, 2 Drummers, and 116 rank and file wounded[33]. General Burgoyne, in a letter written at the time to Lord Derby and subsequently published, says, in reference to Bunker's Hill, "The FIFTH has behaved the best, and suffered the most[34]."

Notwithstanding this success, the army at Boston remained in a state of blockade, and the troops were eventually so distressed for fresh provisions and other necessaries, that live cattle, vegetables, and even fuel, were sent for their use from England. The shipping with these supplies were, however, many of them wrecked, or fell into the hands of the Americans, and, the distress of the troops increasing, much sickness and loss of life occurred.

| 1776 |

In the midst of this calamity, the provincial troops, being better supplied with necessaries, began to act offensively with vigour, and the appearance of new batteries with the opening of a heavy cannonade, occasioned the King's troops to evacuate the place. Accordingly, in the middle of March, 1776, the army embarked from Boston, and proceeded to Halifax in Nova Scotia, but after their arrival at that place the greater part of the troops remained on ship board, the town not being capable of providing quarters, nor of affording a sufficient supply of provisions.

The FIFTH remained at Halifax about two months, and leaving that place early in June to engage in an extensive plan of operations, formed part of the force which effected a landing on Staten Island near New York on the 3rd of July. In the following month a reinforcement of British and Hessian troops arrived, and on the 22nd of August a descent was made on the south-west end of *Long Island*, when the enemy's detachments along the coast withdrew to the range of woody hills which intersect the country from east to west. In the manœuvres by which these hills were passed, and in the defeat of the provincial corps on the 27th of August, the FIFTH took an active and spirited part, but did not sustain any loss. After this success, preparations were made to attack the enemy's lines at *Brooklyn*; but the Americans, impressed with a sense of the superiority of the King's troops, quitted their post during the night of the 28th, and passed the troops in boats across the East River to New York.

The reduction of Long Island having thus been effected with trifling loss, the FIFTH was again embarked, and a landing was made on the 15th of September, on New York Island, within a few miles of the city; which General Washington immediately abandoned, and retired towards the northern end of the island, designing to remain on the defensive, and to avoid a general engagement. The FIFTH was subsequently employed in several operations, and on the 28th of October, being on the march towards the American camp at *White Plains*, it was engaged, with the 28th 35th and 49th regiments, commanded by Brigadier-General Leslie, in forcing the passage of the Brunx's rivulet under a sharp fire, and having ascended the hill with admirable intrepidity, attacked and routed a division of Americans, chasing them from behind walls and other coverts, and driving them behind their entrenchments at the entrance of White Plains: from whence they subsequently retreated. The regiment only lost two men on this occasion, and had its commanding officer, Lieutenant-Colonel Walcott, wounded.

1777

At length, it being found impossible to bring on a general engagement, the army retired by the North River, to the heights of Fordham; and on the 16th of November, the FIFTH supported the storming party in the capture of *Fort Washington*. A few days afterwards the regiment was detached across the North River against *Fort Lee*, and on the flight of the American troops, it was stationed a short time at English Neighbourhood: but was soon called upon to take an active part in the reduction of *New Jersey*; and in the early part of January, 1777, it was quartered at Maidenhead.

The FIFTH passed the remainder of the winter in the island of Jersey. "The weather was particularly severe; the duty unremitting and hard; the enemy watchful; and provisions and forage were not obtained without repeated skirmishes. Nevertheless the soldiers endured these hardships with a fortitude and a perseverance that acquired them infinite honour[35]." The campaign being opened in the early part of June, 1777, the regiment took part in several manœuvres, designed to bring on a general engagement, but the enemy kept in the mountain fastnesses, by which he succeeded in defeating the designs of the British commander; and on the 30th of June the troops embarked from the Jerseys and proceeded to Staten Island.

An expedition to Pennsylvania having been resolved on, the FIFTH formed part of the force ordered for this service, and, having embarked at Sandy Hook on the 5th July, sailed to Chesapeak Bay, thence proceeding up the Elk River, landed at Elk Ferry on the 25th of August, and afterwards advanced on Philadelphia: at the same time the enemy took up a position at *Brandywine Creek*, to oppose the advance. But on the 11th of September the enemy's out-posts were driven in and the position attacked. The FIFTH formed part of the force, which advanced to Chad's Ford in the centre of the enemy's line, forced the passage in gallant style, carried the batteries and intrenchments with fixed bayonets, and captured five pieces of cannon and a howitzer. The regiment encamped during the night on the scene of conflict; its only casualties being Ensign Andrews, 1 serjeant, and 12 men wounded.

This success was followed by the capture of Philadelphia: at the same time the army occupied a position near *Germantown*, and the FIFTH had its post in the right wing of the line. The troops at the head of the town were attacked by the enemy in force at daybreak on the morning of the 4th of October, when the FIFTH was ordered forward to their aid. The enemy had already gained some advantage, and the Fortieth regiment, which had thrown itself into a stone building, was surrounded by an American brigade, when the F<small>IFTH</small> and Fifty-fifth regiments, advancing from the right, opened their fire with good effect, and being seconded by several other corps from the centre and left, drove back the enemy and pursued them through some woody grounds and strong enclosures with signal bravery. The F<small>IFTH</small> lost on this occasion, 1 drummer and 9 men killed; also Lieutenant-Colonel Walcott, Captain Charlton, Ensign Thomas, Ensign Stuart, 5 serjeants, and 37 men wounded: Lieutenant-Colonel Walcott died of his wounds six weeks afterwards.

On the 18th of October the army quitted Germantown and encamped in the immediate vicinity of Philadelphia, until after the capture of two forts on the river. In the mean time the enemy formed a strong camp at White Marsh, fourteen miles from Philadelphia; and in the early part of December the F<small>IFTH</small> took part in several operations and skirmishes designed to bring on a general engagement; but the enemy remaining behind his trenches and *abbatis de bois*, the regiment returned to Philadelphia on the 8th of that month. After the retreat of the King's troops, the enemy removed to Valley Forge, where he built huts and passed the winter in the woods, while the British lay in comfortable quarters in the capital of Pennsylvania, where the want of strict discipline during the period of a temporary repose produced several evil consequences, particularly the estrangement of many persons previously in the interest of the royal cause.

| 1778 |

Before the commencement of active operations in 1778, the King of France had concluded a treaty with, and agreed to aid, the Americans, which so completely changed the nature of the contest, that the evacuation of Philadelphia was resolved upon, and the F<small>IFTH</small> had to take part in the difficult service of retreating through a wild and woody country intersected by rivers, and abounding in narrow and ragged passes. The army accordingly crossed the Delawar on the 18th of June, and directing its march along the eastern bank of that river, afterwards proceeded through the Jerseys, while the enemy hovered near the rear and menaced an attack in force. No action of importance, however, occurred until the 28th of June, when, as the last division descended from the heights above *Freehold* in New Jersey, the enemy appeared in the rear, and on both flanks, and some sharp fighting took place. At this time the F<small>IFTH</small> was in advance, but it was recalled to take part in the action, and the enemy was eventually repulsed. The regiment had Captain Gore of the grenadier company and several men killed on this occasion.

After the action the army continued its march, and having crossed the channel to Sandy Hook, in the beginning of July, embarked from thence for New York; from whence the F<small>IFTH</small> advanced to a post beyond the town.

In September, part of the regiment was detached on an expedition to *Little Egg Harbour* in New Jersey—a noted rendezvous for privateers. This detachment, consisting of 300 men of the F₁FTH and New Jersey Volunteers, commanded by Captain Ferguson, embarked in transports towards the end of September, and, on arriving at the harbour, went on board small vessels which, with several row-galleys, proceeded twenty miles up the river, to Chesnut Neck, where the troops landed under cover of the fire from the galleys, and by a spirited attack, routed the enemy's force assembled to oppose the descent, and chased them into the woods. After returning from the pursuit, the troops destroyed the village, with several storehouses, and armed vessels:—having only sustained the trifling loss of one man of the FIFTH, wounded. A night excursion was afterwards made ten miles farther up the river, when the troops, surprising some companies of the enemy in their quarters, made a dreadful slaughter with the bayonet, and reduced the houses to ashes, with the loss of only two men of the FIFTH killed, and two wounded. "It is but justice to inform you," observes the commanding officer in his despatch, "that the officers and men, both British and Provincials, behaved on this occasion in a manner to do themselves honour. To the conduct and spirit of Captain Cox, Lieutenant Littleton, and Ensign Cotter, of the FIFTH regiment, and of Captain Peter Campbell of the Third Jersey Volunteers, this little enterprise owes much of its success[36]."

Immediately after the return of this detachment, the regiment was ordered to form part of an expedition against the French West India Islands, and embarking on this service under the command of its Lieutenant-Colonel (afterwards Sir William) Medows, sailed from Sandy Hook on the 3rd of November.

After stopping two days at Barbadoes, during which time the land and sea commanders, General James Grant and Admiral Barrington arranged their plans of attack, the expedition arrived at *St. Lucie* on the 13th of December, and the reserve, consisting of the FIFTH regiment, the grenadiers and light infantry being immediately landed under the command of Brigadier-General Medows, forced some heights occupied by a French force under the governor, the Chevalier de Micoud, and took a field-piece and a four-gun battery. On the following morning, the rest of the army being landed, the FIFTH advanced and took possession of the town of Morne Fortuné, the governor's house, hospital and barracks; and from thence, after a short halt, proceeded to occupy an important post, called La Vigie, situated on a tongue of land commanding the north side of the Carenage harbour, and separated by that harbour from the rest of the army. In the mean time, the French fleet under Count D'Estaing arrived off the island, and disembarked a force of nine thousand men, by the whole of which General Medows' little band was attacked on the 18th. The enemy, commanded by MM. de Bouillé and Lavendahl, advanced in three columns; their first two attacks were made, to use the words of General Grant's despatch, "with the impetuosity of Frenchmen, and repulsed with the determined bravery of Britons." They made a third attempt, but were soon broken, and they retired in confusion.

The conduct of the FIFTH regiment and its Lieutenant-Colonel on this occasion, was of the most distinguished description. Brigadier-General Medows, though severely wounded in the right arm early in the day, would not quit his post, but continued in the field, riding about and giving orders, till the attack was over. At one moment, finding his ammunition nearly expended, he drew up his little phalanx in front of their colours, and waving his sword in his hand, emphatically exclaimed, "Soldiers, as long as you have a bayonet to point against an enemy's breast, defend these colours." They did so, and secured the conquest of St. Lucie. It was in this action that the FIFTH by its gallant conduct acquired the privilege of wearing a *White Plume* in the cap instead of the red and white tuft worn by the other regiments of the line; having taken from the bodies of the slain French grenadiers, the advance and élite of the enemy's force, as many white feathers as sufficed to equip every man in the regiment with the new decoration. The loss of the French amounted to about four hundred killed and eleven hundred wounded, while the killed on the side of the British was only ten, and one hundred and thirty wounded; amongst whom were Lieutenants Pratt and Harris. The sense General Grant entertained of the services of Brigadier-General Medows and the detachment under his command, was expressed in the following letter, dated from Morne Fortuné, the 19th of December, 1778:

"Sir,

"I cannot express how much I feel obliged to you, and the troops under your command, for repulsing, with so much spirit and bravery, so great a body of the enemy, and own it was just what I expected from you and them; and I am sure, under your command, they will always behave in such a manner as to do honour to you, themselves, their king, and their country; and I must beg of you to express my gratitude."

1779
1780

During the year 1779, the regiment was sometimes embarked on board ship, and at others employed on shore at St. Lucie and Antigua, and was engaged with the enemy on the 19th of June, 6th of July, and 7th and 8th of September. From January to July, 1780, it was occasionally in Gros Isle Bay, St. Lucie, at Martinique, St. Kitt's, and Carlisle Bay, Barbadoes, and was engaged on the 17th of April, and on the 15th of May. It was then ordered home, and after a boisterous passage, landed on the 16th of September at Portsmouth, from whence it embarked again for Ireland in December, and arrived at Cork in January, 1781.

1781
1782

Towards the end of 1781, a detachment was employed at the mouth of the Shannon, in protecting a foreign vessel, stranded on the coast, from plunder by the natives. The regiment was afterwards quartered at Kilkenny, where its conduct was such that, on its being ordered to a different part of the country, the inhabitants petitioned the Government successfully for its return; at Limerick also, and several other places, its soldier-like and orderly behaviour received the official thanks of the civil authorities. With the volunteers of Ireland, at that time in the height of their popularity and the heyday of their zeal, the FIFTH was on the best footing; whenever it marched through any town, the volunteers turned out to receive it with all due honours, and so great was their respect for the regiment and confidence in its then commander, Lieutenant-Colonel (afterwards Lord) Harris, who had served in the corps from the rank of Ensign upwards, that when, on the report of an intended landing of the French near Cork, the FIFTH was marched to Youghal, several volunteer corps offered to join it in case a landing was effected by the enemy.

1783

In March, 1783, the regiment was marched from Kilkenny to Dublin, and at the first installation of the newly-founded order of St. Patrick, its grenadier company furnished the guard of honour at the Cathedral. A detachment was about the same time sent, under the command of Major Battier, to Carlow, in support of the fencibles, who had been insulted by the volunteers at Kilkenny.

| 1784 |

In 1784, the regiment lost a distinguished leader, a powerful patron, and an attached and sincere friend, by the promotion of Earl Percy to the Colonelcy of the second troop of Horse Grenadier Guards. The F$_{\text{IFTH}}$ had been his first command; he had held that command for sixteen years, including the whole of the American war of independence, and in compliment to him, the regiment had received the denomination, which it still retains, of the "N$_{\text{ORTHUMBERLAND}}$" Regiment. He took leave of his old comrades in the following very complimentary and affectionate letter:—

"Alnwick, Nov. 5, 1784.

"Sir,

"His Majesty having been pleased to appoint me Colonel of the Second Troop of Horse Grenadier Guards, in succession to His Royal Highness Prince Frederick, I take the earliest opportunity of acquainting you with it: and although this new appointment is a very flattering mark of His Majesty's approbation of my services, yet I cannot help feeling the greatest regret at quitting the F$_{\text{IFTH}}$ regiment of Foot, which I have had the pleasure of commanding for sixteen years with great satisfaction to myself, and, I trust, with some advantage to the corps. The very uncommon attention which I have always met with, both from the officers and men of the F$_{\text{IFTH}}$, will ever be remembered by me with the greatest pleasure; and however changed my situation may be with respect to them, my regard, esteem, and affection for them will ever continue the same, and I shall always be happy in having an opportunity of convincing them of it.

"I am, with the greatest regard,
"Yours most sincerely,
(Signed)   "P$_{\text{ERCY}}$.

"Officer commanding F$_{\text{IFTH}}$ Foot."

Earl Percy was succeeded by Major-General the Honourable Edward Stopford, Lieutenant-Colonel of the Sixty-sixth Foot, whose commission as Colonel of the F$_{\text{IFTH}}$ is dated 1st November, 1784.

| 1785 |

The colours of the F$_{\text{IFTH}}$ being worn out by time and numerous honourable perforations received in action, a new set was presented to it with the usual solemnities, on St. George's day, 1785, in the parish church of Belfast, where the regiment was then stationed. In the evening the men dined sumptuously in the barrack-yard by companies, at the expense of their lately promoted

42

Colonel, Earl Percy. In the same year, the assistance rendered by the FIFTH on the occasion of a great fire which broke out in Belfast called forth the public thanks of the corporation and inhabitants.

| 1787 |

The FIFTH remained in Ireland, earning, by its discipline and conduct, the repeated commendations of the several general officers by whom it was commanded or reviewed, till May the 24th, 1787, when it embarked at Monkstown, near Cork, for Canada, and after a voyage of two months, touching by the way at Newfoundland, arrived at Quebec on the 26th of July.

After a short stay at the capital of Lower Canada, the regiment was encamped on the heights above Silleri, and after being reviewed there on the 29th of August, 1787, by his Royal Highness Prince William Henry (afterwards King William IV.), was embarked at Wolfe's Cove on the 6th of September, in batteaux, for the interior, where it remained for nine years.

| 1790 |
| 1791 |

From June, 1790, to the same month in 1792, it was quartered at Detroit, on the Straits of St. Clair, above Lake Erie, in Upper Canada. While the regiment was at this station, under the command of Lieutenant-Colonel Smith[37]; the first aggression was made by the troops of the United States on the Indian territory; and his humane interference and exertions rescued many Americans from the Indians, into whose hands they had fallen, for which he received the thanks of the President.

| 1792 |

From Detroit the regiment moved, in June, 1792, down to Niagara, where it was reviewed by his Royal Highness the Duke of Kent and Major-General Simcoe, who made a highly favourable report of it to the Commander-in-Chief, declaring it to be "most fit for actual service." From Niagara, Lieutenant Sheaffe[38] of the FIFTH, was detached to coast the shore of Lake Ontario, and protest against the settlements made by the Americans at Sodius, and other places, during the suspended execution of the first American treaty.

| 1794 |

General Stopford died in 1794, and was succeeded in the Colonelcy of the FIFTH, by Sir Alured Clarke, G.C.B., whose commission was dated the 25th of October, in that year. The regiment was still at Niagara, where it remained till that post was given up to the Americans in 1796, when it was ordered to Quebec.

| 1796 |
| 1797 |

In the winter of 1796 it was employed against the insurgent Canadians at Point Levi, on which occasion it crossed the St. Lawrence on the ice. In 1797, the corporals and privates were drafted into the Twenty-fourth regiment, while the officers and serjeants returned to England, and on their disembarkation were ordered to Grantham, in Lincolnshire, to recruit; which service was very successfully carried on in all the principal towns of the county. From Grantham it was moved to Boston, and from thence suddenly ordered to Norman Cross barracks, where some disturbances had broken out among the French prisoners. After a few months, however, at the particular request of the inhabitants of Boston, it was again quartered in that town, on which occasion the volunteer corps lined the streets through which the regiment had to pass, and a splendid dinner and ball were given to the officers by the inhabitants. This kindly feeling between Lincolnshire and the FIFTH regiment has continued ever since, and more recruits have joined its ranks from that county than from any other.

When the expedition sent out with the view of delivering Holland from the power of France was determined on in 1799, the FIFTH regiment, already in a high state of efficiency, both with respect to numbers and discipline, was selected to form part of the army destined for that service, and was accordingly marched to the camp on Barham Downs. It was immediately after divided into two battalions, upwards of eight hundred each, in strength, Major-General George Hewett being appointed on the 5th of August, 1799, Colonel-Commandant of the second battalion; and in September both battalions embarked at Deal for Holland, where they landed on the 14th and 15th, and formed with the Thirty-fifth regiment, the eighth brigade of the army, under the command of His Royal Highness Prince William of Gloucester.

In the general attack made on the 19th of September on the whole line of the French positions in North Holland, the FIFTH regiment formed part of the column under Lieutenant-General Dundas, destined to carry the intrenched villages of *Walmenhuysen*, and *Schoreldam*, in the attack upon the latter of which, the first battalion took an active part, and had one Lieutenant (Harris) mortally, and its Lieutenant-Colonel (Stephenson) severely wounded; sustaining, besides, a loss of five killed, four wounded, and four missing. Of this action the Duke of York observed, in his public despatch, "The gallantry displayed by the troops engaged, the spirit with which they overcame every obstacle which nature and art opposed to them, and the cheerfulness with which they maintained the fatigue of an action, which lasted without

44

intermission, from half-past three o'clock in the morning, until five in the afternoon, are beyond my power to describe or extol. Their exertions fully entitle them to the admiration and gratitude of their King and country."

In the battle of *Egmont-op-Zee* on the 2nd and 6th of October, Prince William's brigade was not actively engaged; but the flank companies of the FIFTH, which were attached to the grenadier and light infantry battalions of the line, and formed part of the reserve under Colonel Macdonald of the Fifty- fifth regiment, had an opportunity of distinguishing themselves; they had several men killed and wounded, also Captain Pratt wounded on the 2nd, and Lieutenant Hamilton on the 6th of October; and on both occasions behaved so well as to receive the particular thanks of their commander.

On the 10th of October the posts occupied by the two battalions of the FIFTH, in front of the village of *Winkle*, were attacked by the enemy in great strength. The French troops had succeeded in forcing a passage over a canal which covered the village, when Colonel Bligh, who commanded the first battalion, perceiving that if the advance of the enemy was not checked, the remainder of the brigade was in danger of being cut off, planted the colours of the FIFTH on the top of the dyke, and kept his ground till he had secured and covered the retreat of the brigade; the second battalion, under Lieutenant-Colonel Talbot, in the mean time maintaining its positions till ordered to retreat by Prince William, who on this occasion, issued the following general order:—

"Oude, Sluys, 12th October, 1799.

"Prince William desires Colonel Bligh and the first battalion of the *Fifth* Regiment will accept his thanks, for the gallant manner in which they attacked the enemy when he was passing the canal opposite Winkle; and Lieutenant-Colonels Talbot and Lindsay, of the second battalion of the FIFTH, for their exertions on the 10th instant."

1800

The Dutch did not second the gallant exertions thus made to effect their deliverance from foreign domination, and the evacuation of Holland was resolved on. As late as the 12th of October, the FIFTH Regiment was still in front of the enemy, and eventually occupied the works at the Helder, during the retreat and final embarkation of the army; being, according to Sir James Pulteney's letter of the 20th of November, among the last of the British troops who quitted Holland, and exhibiting to the end, persevering good conduct and unwearied courage, under hardships which his Royal Highness the Duke of York, in general orders, dated 8th of October, 1799, designated as "insupportable." On its arrival in England, the regiment was stationed at

Silver Hill barracks, and the following year both battalions were ordered to Gibraltar.

| 1801 |

In August, 1801, Sir Alured Clarke was removed to the Colonelcy of the Seventh Foot, and the command of the FIFTH was bestowed on the 20th of August, on Major-General Richard England, who, from the 14th of April, 1800, had been Colonel-Commandant of the second battalion.

| 1802 |
| 1803 |
| 1804 |

At Gibraltar the regiment continued till the peace of Amiens, when it returned to England. The second battalion was then disbanded at Winchester, and the first ordered to Guernsey, where it remained till 1804, when it returned to England, and was stationed first, for a short time, at Hilsea, and afterwards at Colchester. The war with France having been resumed, a second battalion was again raised, in 1804, and embodied at Horsham in Sussex.

| 1805 |

In 1805, the establishment of the first battalion was augmented to 1000 rank and file; and it was, with other regiments, reviewed in the autumn at Colchester, by his Royal Highness the Duke of York.

In the same year the second battalion was stationed at Chichester, and recruited successfully in Petworth, Steyning, Midhurst, Lewes, and Rye; in February, 1806, it was sent to Guernsey, and from thence in August following, it was removed to Alderney.

| 1806 |

In November, 1805, the first battalion embarked at Deal, with the forces under Lord Cathcart, destined for the defence of Hanover. During the voyage the "Helder" transport, containing the left wing of the battalion, was unfortunately wrecked off the Helder, and the officers and men were made prisoners by the Dutch. The right wing returned to England in 1806, and was stationed at Rye, in Sussex, where it was joined in September, by the left wing, which had been liberated by an exchange of prisoners.

| 1807 |

In 1806, the first battalion sailed in the expedition under Brigadier-General Robert Craufurd, to join the British forces at Monte Video, in the province of Buenos Ayres, in South America; and after being embarked upwards of nine months, landed on the 28th of June, 1807, at Ensenada de Barragon, and was formed in Brigadier-General Sir Samuel Achmuty's brigade, for the attack

46

made by Lieutenant-General Whitelocke, on the capital of the province.

After some fatiguing marches through a country much intersected by swamps and deep muddy rivulets, the troops crossed the Rio Chuelo, and formed in the suburbs of *Buenos Ayres*, when the F<small>IFTH</small> had its post towards the convent of Recoleta; and in the plan for the general attack, the regiment was formed in two divisions, and directed to penetrate the streets immediately in its front. Accordingly, at half-past six o'clock on the morning of the 5th of July, the regiment advanced: the streets were found deserted by the inhabitants; the houses and shops closed; and a death-like silence, interrupted only by the firm tread of the British soldier, reigned in the midst of this populous city; but at a given signal, the whole male population suddenly appeared, and the windows and tops of the flat-roofed houses were crowded with armed men, who commenced a destructive fire; at the same time the streets were found intersected by ditches, and protected by cannon; but the F<small>IFTH</small>, pressing onward with a conquering might which overcame all resistance, forced its passage through the streets with fixed bayonets, and, after penetrating to the river, took possession of the church and convent of St. Catalina, from whence it moved to the Plaza de Toros, where thirty-two pieces of cannon and a quantity of ammunition were captured. In the mean time several other corps, not able to overcome the opposition they met with, had been repulsed or overpowered, and made prisoners by the Spaniards; and on the following day Lieutenant-General Whitelocke agreed to vacate the place. In this affair the F<small>IFTH</small> sustained a loss of fourteen killed, also forty-seven wounded, amongst the latter was Major the Honourable Henry King; and twenty-four missing. On the conclusion of the treaty between General Whitelocke and General Liniers, the English army re-embarked, and, after a tedious voyage, during which it was exposed to considerable want both of provisions and water, the 1st battalion of the F<small>IFTH</small> Regiment landed at Cork, in December, 1807, where the 2nd battalion also arrived from Alderney on the 3rd of the same month.

In the same year, the sanction of his Royal Highness the Prince Regent was obtained for clothing the drummers of the regiment in white, with white and red lace, instead of gosling green.

| 1808 |

The second battalion was quartered at Charles Fort, Kinsale, from whence it marched in February, 1808, to Fermoy. In the summer of the same year, the first battalion, under the command of Lieutenant-Colonel John Mackenzie, was ordered to proceed to the aid of the Portuguese in their resistance to the tyrannical power of Buonaparte; it accordingly embarked at Cork, and sailed on the 12th July for Portugal; where it landed on the 9th of August, and immediately joined the army of Lieutenant-General Sir Arthur Wellesley. In the action at *Roleia*, on the 17th, it was one of the few corps whom circumstances and the nature of the ground permitted to come to actual engagement with the enemy; and advancing by the right-hand path to the heights of Zambugeira, it climbed the rugged rocks in the face of a French force, which, after a gallant resistance, was driven from the heights. Thus by its conduct on that day, wherein two of its officers, Major Emes and Lieutenant Doyle were wounded, it earned the Royal permission to have the word "R$_{OLEIA}$" inscribed on its colours. Its further loss was three killed, and two serjeants and thirty-nine rank and file wounded. Sir Arthur Wellesley, in his despatch, observed, "I cannot sufficiently applaud the conduct of the troops throughout this action. The enemy's positions were formidable, and he took them up with his usual ability and celerity, and defended them most gallantly. I must observe, that although we had such a superiority of numbers employed in the operations of this day, the troops actually engaged in the heat of the action were, from unavoidable circumstances, only the F$_{IFTH}$, Ninth, Twenty-ninth, the riflemen of the Sixtieth and Ninety-fifth, and the flank companies of Major-General Hill's brigade, being in number by no means equal to that of the enemy;—their conduct therefore deserves the highest commendation."

In the subsequent battle of *Vimiera*, fought on the 21st of August, the first battalion of the F$_{IFTH}$ forming, with the Ninth and Thirty-eighth Regiments, the first brigade, was posted on the mountain on the right of the village. The enemy was defeated, and the regiment was rewarded by royal permission to inscribe the word "V$_{IMIERA}$" also upon its colours.

These successes being followed by the Convention of Cintra, and the evacuation of Portugal by the French, the first battalion of the F$_{IFTH}$ was afterwards stationed in Lisbon, where it remained several weeks.

Portugal being now free from the presence of an enemy, an army, commanded by Lieutenant-General Sir John Moore, was sent up the country in the autumn, to assist the Spaniards in their resistance to the armies of France, and the first battalion of the F$_{IFTH}$ Regiment was selected to form part of this expedition.

| 1809 |

Passing through Portugal by a rapid march, the troops traversed four hundred miles in a short time, and were soon engaged in operations in Spain; but the Spaniards, who were to have co-operated, had in the mean time been defeated and dispersed; and the little British army was eventually obliged to retire before the superior numbers of the enemy. The F$_{IFTH}$ Regiment took its full share in the disasters and privations of the retreat from Sahagun to

Corunna, as well as in the glories of the 16th of January, 1809, when the steady firmness of the British army, by repulsing at all points an assailant, superior in numbers and artillery, and commanded by one of the ablest generals[39] that France could boast, proved to the world that even a forced retreat of two hundred and fifty miles, made under circumstances the most disheartening, and accompanied by privations the most appalling, though it might wear the sinews and exhaust the physical strength of the British soldier, had no power to shake his resolution or daunt his courage.

In the battle of *Corunna*, Colonel Mackenzie particularly distinguished himself: after having one horse shot under him, he remounted another, and was at length mortally wounded, whereupon the command of the battalion devolved on Major Emes, who received a medal for this service, while the regiment itself acquired another honorary inscription for its colours, 'CORUNNA' being by royal permission borne upon them. The number of killed and wounded of the first battalion of the FIFTH, in the battle of Corunna, has never been exactly ascertained; but on mustering after its return to England, one serjeant, two corporals, three drummers, and one hundred and twenty-six rank and file were found to be missing.

The first battalion landed in February, 1809, at Ramsgate, and after a halt of a few days at Margate, was ordered to Steyning, in Sussex, where it was fully equipped and completed to upwards of one thousand rank and file, and embarked in July following at Portsmouth, under the command of Lieutenant-Colonel Pratt, to form part of the expedition under the Earl of Chatham designed to effect the destruction of the enemy's shipping and arsenal on the Scheldt.

During the siege of *Flushing*, on the Island of Walcheren, the first battalion of the FIFTH was very actively employed, and although bivouacked without tents during the whole time (with the exception of one week that it was in garrison in Flushing, after its surrender) had very few sick; but on being embarked to proceed up the Scheldt for the projected attack upon Antwerp, the Walcheren fever broke out in its ranks with dreadful violence, attacking about six hundred men. In the active operations it lost one captain (Talbot) killed, and Captain M. Hamilton and Lieutenant Galbraith were wounded, the former losing a leg: its loss from disease was much more severe, for before its return to England, in December following, two captains (Philips and William Hamilton), and three lieutenants (Brown, MacDonough, and Cary) and many men had been carried off by the fever. On its return to England, the battalion was stationed at Bexhill.

In the mean time a detachment of the regiment left in Portugal, when the first battalion advanced into Spain, had been added to a battalion of detachments under Lieutenant-Colonel Copson of the F$_{\text{IFTH}}$, and warmly engaged at the battle of *Talavera*, on the 27th and 28th of July, for which Lieutenant-Colonel Copson received a medal.

The second battalion had been removed from Fermoy, in April of this year, to Coloony in the King's County, and from thence in June to Cork, and, embarking at Cove, landed on the 4th of July at Lisbon; and on the 3rd of August marched, under command of Lieutenant-Colonel the Honourable Henry King, to join the army in the field under Lieutenant-General Sir Arthur Wellesley, and take its share in the subsequent operations of the campaign. About the end of September it was reinforced by nearly one hundred men of the first battalion, who had been left behind as before stated, and it passed the winter in quarters near the Portuguese frontiers.

| 1810 |

The immense preparations of the enemy for the ensuing campaign induced Lord Wellington[40] to limit his operations in 1810 to the defence of Portugal. The second battalion of the F$_{\text{IFTH}}$ formed part of Major-General Lightburn's brigade of the third (Sir Thomas Picton's) division of the army, and was stationed for some time behind the Mondego river, from whence it advanced to Pinhel behind the Coa to support the light division; and was afterwards employed in a series of operations to retard the advance of the overpowering numbers of the enemy. At length Lord Wellington made a stand on the rocks of *Busaco*; and the third division had its post on the heights near the village of St. Antonio de Cantara. Here the second battalion of the F$_{\text{IFTH}}$ was first under fire, and its light company, under Lieutenant Shadwell Clerke, was thrown out to repulse the advancing skirmishers of the enemy, a service which it most promptly and gallantly performed.

The French, after astonishing efforts, gave way before the superior valour and tactics of the British troops. For this victory, Lieutenant-Colonel the Honourable Henry King, commanding the battalion, received a medal, and the word "B$_{\text{USACO}}$" was authorized, on the 31st of December, 1825, to be inscribed upon the colours of the regiment. Its loss in the battle of Busaco was one killed and seven wounded.

After the battle, the French having made a flank movement, Lord Wellington retired to the celebrated lines of *Torres Vedras*, where he posed an insurmountable barrier to the further progress of the enemy; and the second battalion of the F$_{\text{IFTH}}$ passed the remainder of the year in these stupendous works.

The first battalion remaining on home service was removed, in March, 1810, from Bexhill to Lewes, and on the 12th of August was, with several other corps, reviewed on Brighton Downs by his Royal Highness the Prince Regent, attended by his Royal Highness the Duke of Clarence, (afterwards King William IV.,) who expressed themselves in terms of approbation of its appearance and discipline. Two days afterwards the battalion marched to Portsmouth, where it embarked for Ireland, and on its arrival was quartered at Fermoy.

| 1811 |

During the early part of 1811, the second battalion remained in the lines of Torres Vedras, where Major-General the Honourable Charles Colville took command of the brigade. The enemy, defeated in his purpose, reduced in numbers by sickness, and in want of provisions, was obliged to retreat; and the second battalion of the F<small>IFTH</small>, moving with its division from the lines, was employed in the pursuit of Marshal Massena towards the frontiers of Portugal. It was frequently engaged with the enemy's rear guards, and on the 12th of March had a sharp affair at *Redinha*, where, descending from the woody heights on the enemy's left, it cleared the grounds in its front in fine style, and forded a deep and rapid river, under the fire of the enemy, when Lieutenant Clerke, already mentioned as commanding the light company at Busaco, was severely wounded in the leg, which he lost in consequence.

The battalion continued to take an active part in the pursuit; and in the action at *Sabugal*, on the 3rd of April, it forded the river Coa, and immediately afterwards, on ascending the heights, and while the brigade was forming on one of the centre companies of the F<small>IFTH</small>, the skirmishers were rapidly driven in. The F<small>IFTH</small>, commanded by Major Ridge, suddenly found itself in presence of a strong French column, upon which it instantly advanced, opening at the same time a heavy fire; the enemy was repulsed with severe loss, and driven precipitately, and in the greatest disorder, down the hill. In this affair Lieutenant Sinclair was killed, and Ensign Williams, one serjeant, and five rank and file, wounded.

Almeida having been blockaded by the British, the French advanced to relieve the place, and crossed the frontiers of Portugal on the 2nd of May. On that day the battalion of the F<small>IFTH</small> was again in sight of the enemy, and on the 5th of the same month it was present, under the command of Lieutenant-Colonel King (who had rejoined), at the battle of *Fuentes d'Onor*, where the enemy was defeated, and his design to relieve Almeida frustrated. In this action the battalion had four rank and file wounded.

Immediately after the battle of Fuentes d'Onor, the second battalion of the F<small>IFTH</small> was detached to the south to join the forces under Marshal Beresford, and it was employed in the second siege of *Badajoz*, where it was one of the first corps to break ground. In the operations of this siege, which was raised on the morning of the 17th of June, Lieutenant Sedgwick of the F<small>IFTH</small> (acting as engineer) and three rank and file were killed, and one serjeant and three rank and file were wounded.

Returning to the north, the battalion commanded by Major Ridge was stationed, during the month of August and part of September, in the village of Fuente Guinaldo, then the head-quarters of Lord Wellington: it was the only British corps in the village, and was considered such a favourite as to have acquired the *nom de guerre* of "Lord Wellington's body-guard."

It was afterwards employed in the blockade of Ciudad Rodrigo; and on the 24th of September it was ordered to a position on the heights near the village of *El Bodon*, on the left of the Agueda and within a few miles of Ciudad Rodrigo. The enemy, having assembled an immense force to relieve the place, advanced on the morning of the 25th, and the second battalion of the F<small>IFTH</small> sustained an attack from a vastly superior French force, consisting of cavalry, infantry, and artillery, in so distinguished a manner, that its conduct was held up in General Orders as an example to the whole army. The behaviour of the battalion on this proud occasion is described by Lord Wellington in his public despatch as follows:—

"The enemy's attention was principally directed during this day (the 25th) to the portion of the third division on the hills between Fuente Guinaldo and Pastores. About eight in the morning they moved a column, consisting of between thirty and forty squadrons of cavalry, and fourteen battalions of infantry, and twelve pieces of cannon, from Ciudad Rodrigo, in such a direction that it was doubtful whether they would attempt to ascend the hills by Encina, El Bodon, or by the direct road towards Fuente Guinaldo, and I was not certain by which road they would make their attack till they actually commenced it upon the last. As soon as I saw the direction of their march, I had reinforced the second battalion of the F<small>IFTH</small> regiment, which occupied the post on the hill, over which the road passes to Guinaldo, by the Seventy-seventh regiment, and by the Twenty-first Portuguese regiment, under the command of Major-General the Honourable Charles Colville, and Major-General Alten's brigade, of which only three squadrons remained, which had not been detached, drawn from El Bodon, and I ordered there a brigade of the fourth division, from Fuente Guinaldo, and afterwards from El Bodon the remainder of the troops of the third division, with the exception of those at Pastores, which were too distant. In the mean time, however, the small body of troops at this post sustained the attack of the enemy's cavalry and artillery. One regiment of French dragoons succeeded in taking two pieces of cannon, which had been posted on a rising ground on the right of our troops; but they were charged by the second battalion of the F$_{\text{IFTH}}$ regiment, under the command of Major Ridge, and the guns were immediately re-taken.

"While this operation was going on on the flank, an attack was made on the front by another regiment, which was repulsed in a similar manner by the Seventy-seventh regiment, and the three squadrons of Major-General Alten's brigade charged repeatedly different bodies of the enemy, which ascended the hill on the left of the two regiments of British infantry, the Portuguese regiment being posted in the rear of their right.

"At length the division of the enemy's infantry, which had marched with the cavalry from Ciudad Rodrigo, was brought up to the attack on the road to Fuente Guinaldo. The second battalion of the F$_{\text{IFTH}}$ regiment, and the Seventy-seventh regiment, were formed into one square, and the Twenty-first Portugese regiment into another, supported by Major-General Alten's small body of cavalry and the Portuguese artillery.

"The enemy's cavalry immediately rushed forward, and obliged our cavalry to retire to the support of the Portuguese regiment, and the F$_{\text{IFTH}}$ and Seventy-seventh regiments were charged, on three faces of the square, by the French cavalry, but they halted and repulsed the attack with the utmost steadiness and gallantry. We then continued the retreat, and joined the remainder of the third division, also formed in squares, on their march to Fuente Guinaldo; and the whole retired together in the utmost order, and the enemy never made another attempt to charge any of them, but were satisfied with firing upon them with their artillery, and with following them.

"I cannot conclude this report of the occurrence of the last week, without expressing to your Lordship my admiration of the conduct of the troops engaged in the affair of the 25th instant. The conduct of the second battalion of the F$_{\text{IFTH}}$ regiment, commanded by Major Ridge, in particular, affords a memorable example of what the steadiness and discipline of the troops, and their confidence in their officers, can effect, in the most difficult and trying situations. The conduct of the Seventy-seventh regiment under Lieutenant-Colonel Bromhead was equally good; and I have never seen a more determined attack than was made by the whole of the enemy's cavalry, with every advantage of the assistance of a superior artillery, and repulsed by these two weak battalions."

The following are extracts from General Orders issued by command of Lord Wellington on this memorable occasion.

"Head-Quarters, Regidsa, 2nd October, 181 .

No. 3. "The commander of the forces is desirous of drawing the attention of the army to the conduct of the second battalion of the Fᴵꜰᴛʜ regiment, and Seventy-seventh regiment, and Twenty-first Portuguese regiment, and Major Arentschildt's Portuguese artillery, under the command of the Honourable Major-General Colville, and of the Eleventh Light Dragoons and First Hussars, under Major-General Alten, in the affair with the enemy on the 25th of September ultimo. These troops were attacked by between thirty and forty squadrons of cavalry, with six pieces of cannon, supported by a division, consisting of fourteen battalions of infantry, with cannon."

No. 4. "The Portuguese artillery-men were cut down at their guns before they would quit them; but the second battalion of the Fᴵꜰᴛʜ regiment attacked the cavalry, which had taken their guns, and retook them; at the same time the Seventy-seventh regiment was attacked in front by another body of cavalry, upon which body they advanced, and repulsed them."

No. 5. "While those actions were performed, Major-General Alten's brigade, of which there were only three squadrons on the ground, was engaged on the left with numbers infinitely superior to themselves. These squadrons charged repeatedly, supporting each other, and took about twenty prisoners, and, notwithstanding the immense superiority of the enemy, the post would have been maintained, if the commander of the forces had not ordered the troops to withdraw from it, seeing that the action would have been still more unequal, as the enemy's infantry were likely to be engaged in it before the reinforcements ordered to support the post could arrive."

No. 6. "The troops then retired with the same determined spirit, and in the same good order, with which they had maintained their post—the second battalion of the Fᴵꜰᴛʜ and Seventy-seventh regiments in one square, and the Twenty-first Portuguese in another, supported by Major-General's Alten's cavalry, and the Portuguese artillery. The enemy's cavalry charged three faces of the square of the British infantry, but were beaten off; and, finding from their fruitless efforts that those brave troops were not to be broken, they were content with following them at a distance, and firing upon them with artillery, till the troops joined the remainder of the third division, and were afterwards supported by a brigade of the fourth division. Although the Twenty-first Portuguese regiment was not actually charged by the enemy's cavalry, their steadiness and determination were conspicuous, and the commander of the forces observed with pleasure the order and regularity with which they made all their movements, and the confidence they showed in their officers."

No. 7. "The commander of the forces has been particular in stating the details of this action in the general orders, as in his opinion it affords a memorable example of what can be effected by steadiness, discipline, and confidence. It is impossible that any troops can be exposed at any time to the attack of numbers relatively greater than those which attacked the troops under Major-General Colville and Major-General Alten, on the 25th of September; and the commander of the forces recommends the conduct of these troops to the particular attention of the officers and soldiers of the army, as an example to be followed in all such circumstances."

No. 8. "The commander of the forces considers Major-General Alten and Major-General Colville, and the commanding officers of regiments under their command respectively, *viz.* Lieutenant-Colonel Cummins, Lieutenant-Colonel Arentschildt, Lieutenant-Colonel Bromhead, Major Ridge, and Colonel Bucella, of the Twenty-first Portuguese, and the officers and soldiers under their command, to be entitled to his particular thanks, and assures them that he has not failed to report his sense of their conduct, in the action of the 25th of September, to those by whom he trusts that it will be duly appreciated and recollected."

Further eulogium, or even comment, on the brilliant conduct of the second battalion of this regiment at E<small>L</small> B<small>ODON</small> it must be felt, is unnecessary, and would be supererogatory: its loss was five rank and file killed, and Captain Ramus, one serjeant, and twelve rank and file, wounded. The army moved forward on the 26th to occupy other positions, and the battalion, for the remainder of 1811, was posted in the village of Payo, near the pass of Perales.

| 1812 |

The first operation of the year 1812 was the siege of *Ciudad Rodrigo*, in the storming of which fortress, on the 19th of January, the second battalion of the F<small>IFTH</small> had another glorious opportunity of distinguishing itself and earning one more honourable inscription for the regimental colours. On this occasion, moving from its post behind the convent of Santa Cruz, it entered the ditch at the extremity of the counterscarp, then, after escalading the wall and scouring the *fausse braye* to the great breach, it rushed forward in the face of a thundering discharge of shells, grape, and musketry, which thinned the ranks; yet, continuing its course with unabated fury, it drove the French, with fixed bayonets, behind the entrenchments. Here the enemy rallied, some hard fighting occurred, but at length the British, by a mighty effort, burst through the entrenchment. In the mean time the other attacks had also succeeded. The garrison fought for a moment in the streets; but eventually fled to the castle and surrendered. The Commander-in-Chief, in his despatch to the Earl of Liverpool, dated Gallegos, 20th of January, 1812, says:—

"Major Ridge, of the second battalion, F<small>IFTH</small> regiment, having escaladed the *fausse braye* wall, stormed the principal breach in the body of the place, together with the Ninety-fourth regiment[41], commanded by Lieutenant-Colonel Campbell, which had moved along the ditch at the same time, and had stormed the breach in the *fausse braye*, both in front of Major-General Mackinnon's brigade. Thus these regiments not only effectually covered the advance from the trenches of Major-General Mackinnon's brigade by their first movements and operations, but they preceded them in the attack.

"The conduct of all parts of the third division in the operations which they performed with so much gallantry and exactness, on the evening of the 19th in the dark, affords the strongest proof of the abilities of Lieutenant-General Picton and Major-General Mackinnon, by whom they were directed and led; but I beg particularly to draw your lordship's attention to the conduct of Lieutenant-Colonel O'Toole, of the second Caçadores; of Major Ridge, second battalion FIFTH Foot; of Lieutenant-Colonel Campbell, Ninety-fourth regiment; of Major Manners, of the Seventy-fourth; and of Major Grey, second battalion FIFTH Foot, who has been twice wounded during the siege."

The loss of the battalion during the siege, and at the storming of Ciudad Rodrigo, was heavy, Captain McDougal, one serjeant, and thirty-four rank and file, being killed, and Major Grey, Captain Dubourdieu, Lieutenants Wylde, McKenzie, D. E. Johnson, Fitzgerald, and Fairtclough, Ensigns Ashford and Canch (who carried the colours at the assault), and Volunteer Hillyard, with three serjeants, and fifty-five rank and file, wounded. Major Ridge obtained the rank of Lieutenant-Colonel, and the words 'CIUDAD RODRIGO' are authorized, under date October the 25th, 1817, to be borne on the colours of the regiment.

As soon as the breaches in Ciudad Rodrigo were repaired, and the place put in a state of defence, the Earl of Wellington undertook, for a third time, the siege of *Badajoz*, and on the 16th of March the second battalion of the FIFTH, with the remainder of Sir Thomas Picton's division, having marched to the Alentejo, crossed the Guadiana, and took up its position in the investing force. In the assault, which took place at ten o'clock on the night of the 6th of April, General Picton's division was directed to file out of the trenches, cross the Rivillas river, and scale the castle walls, which were from eighteen to twenty-four feet high; furnished with all means of destruction, and so narrow at the top that the defenders could easily overturn the ladders. The second battalion of the FIFTH led the brigade to which it belonged, and, passing the Rivillas by a narrow bridge under a hot fire of musketry, the troops reared their ladders against the lofty castle, and with undaunted courage ascended amidst a shower of heavy stones, logs of wood, and bursting shells from the parapet, while the enemy plied a heavy fire from the flanks, and with pikes or bayonets stabbed the leading assailants in front, or pushed the ladders from the wall. Yet, amidst the deafening noise of musketry, the crash of breaking ladders, and the sound of falling weights, the men were seen striving who should first ascend, until, all being overturned, a pause ensued, and the French shouted "Victory."—A vain shout:—for in a few moments the heroic Lieutenant-Colonel Ridge, who commanded the FIFTH, springing forward, and calling on his men to follow, raised a ladder against the castle on the right of the former attack, Ensign Canch raised a second, and the next moment these two, with Colonel Campbell of the Ninety-fourth (commanding the brigade), followed by the grenadiers, were on the rampart. The remainder of the men followed cheering, and, when a sufficient number had succeeded in gaining the summit of the wall, the gallant Ridge, calling out "Come on, my lads, let us be the first to seize the governor," led them along the ramparts and drove the garrison before them with terrible slaughter through the double gate into the town. The enemy sent a reinforcement, but it was driven back. Thus the castle was nobly won, and the grenadiers of the FIFTH had the honour of having led the successful escalade, under circumstances which gave an interesting character to this daring exploit. A shot in the breast unfortunately closed the mortal career of Lieutenant-Colonel Ridge even in the moment of victory, and deprived the regiment, and the service in general, of a most valuable officer[42]. His family had the melancholy satisfaction of receiving the medal which, had he survived, would have graced his own breast: another medal was given to Major Bishop, who, on the death of his Lieutenant-Colonel, succeeded to the temporary command of the battalion; and, in reward and commemoration of its services on this occasion, the word "BADAJOZ" is, by authority dated July the 4th, 1818, borne on the colours. During the siege and assault, the battalion lost, besides its lamented Lieutenant-Colonel, one Lieutenant (Fairtclough), one serjeant, and sixteen rank and file, killed; and two captains, Bennett (aide-de-camp to Major-General Kempt) and Doyle, Lieutenant John Pennington, and Ensign Hopkins, with three serjeants, and twenty-seven rank and file, wounded.

After the capture of Badajoz, the second battalion accompanied the army towards the north of Portugal and into Spain; it was in position on the heights of St. Christoval until after the capture of the forts at Salamanca. It was afterwards in position on the Douro, and was for a time posted, with the remainder of the third division, to observe the ford of Pollos, while the opposite bank of the river was occupied by the French army; and it was occasionally under the enemy's fire in the course of the movements which preceded the battle of Salamanca.

During this period, the first battalion, which had embarked at Cork in May, landed at Lisbon, and, advancing by forced marches, joined the army about the 20th of July, a few leagues in front of Salamanca, taking the right of that brigade of the third division which had been hitherto formed by the second battalion of the FIFTH, the Eighty-third, and the Ninety-fourth regiments.

The two battalions of the FIFTH were thus united in time for the whole regiment to share in the honours and triumphs of the 22nd of July, 1812, the glorious victory of *Salamanca*. In the course of this day, while the French were manœuvring, the third division, being suddenly ordered to cross their line of march, sprang forward with an energy and force which broke the half-formed French lines into fragments, and drove them in confusion upon the support. The shock of this gallant and unexpected attack threw the enemy into confusion; and the division continuing its spirited advance, the right flank of the first battalion of the FIFTH was threatened by a charge of cavalry, when three companies were thrown back *en potence*, and, coolly allowing the enemy's horse to advance so close that every shot would tell, opened so steady and well-directed a fire, that they were instantly repulsed, and they fled in disorder. The division again bearing onwards in its victorious course, its attack was rendered decisive by a brilliant charge of the heavy cavalry; and finally the enemy sustained an entire overthrow. Lieutenant-Colonel Pratt, of the first battalion, Lieutenant-Colonel the Honourable Henry King, of the second (who in the course of the day succeeded to the temporary command of the brigade), and Captain Bishop (on whom at the same time the temporary command of the second battalion devolved), obtained medals; and the good conduct of the regiment in general was rewarded by authority, under date October the 25th, 1817, to bear the word "SALAMANCA" inscribed on its colours. Its loss amounted to one serjeant and ten rank and file killed; and Captain Simcocks, Lieutenants Bird, McPherson, O'Dell, Gunn, Hamilton, and Hillyard, Ensign Pratt, and eleven serjeants, one drummer, and one hundred and nineteen rank and file, wounded.

The loss of the second battalion in the brilliant but severe service in which it had now for three years[43] been constantly engaged was so serious, that, on the arrival of the army in Madrid, the capture of which capital was the first fruit of the victory of Salamanca, it was ordered to England to recruit its thinned ranks. After transferring the effective privates to the first battalion, it took leave of the army at Madrid on the 3rd of September, embarked at Lisbon in November, and on the 1st of December landed at Plymouth, from whence it marched, on the following day, to Kingsbridge, to join its depôt, and finally, in January, 1813, took up its quarters in Exeter. The estimation in which this battalion was held by the Earl of Wellington will be best shown by the following extracts from general orders, dated Arcala, July 27th, 1812.

"The Commander of the Forces cannot part with the officers and non-commissioned officers of the second battalion of the F<small>IFTH</small> regiment, without again requesting them to accept his thanks for their uniform good conduct and brilliant and important services since they have been under his command."

The first battalion remained stationary in Madrid, while the Marquis of Wellington marched with part of the army and commenced the siege of Burgos; and, when the advance of the enemy's immense force rendered a retreat necessary, the battalion marched on the 24th of October, with the rest of the third division, to join the army, then retiring from the siege, and, returning with it into Portugal, was stationed for the winter in the villages of Ferrerina and Faya.

Lieutenant-General Richard England died on the 7th of November this year, and on the 27th of the same month Major-General William Wynyard, from the Royal West India Rangers, was appointed to the Colonelcy of this regiment.

1813

On the 16th of May, 1813, the first battalion of the F<small>IFTH</small> broke up from its cantonments, and (brigaded with the Eighty-third, Eighty-seventh, and Ninety-fourth, under the Honourable Sir Charles Colville,) advanced with the rest of the army into Spain. At the memorable and decisive battle of *Vittoria*, it forded the river, and advancing against the right of the French army at Margarita and Hermanded, displayed its usual spirit and intrepidity, driving in a superior force of the enemy in gallant style. The Marquis of Wellington, in his despatch, notices the conduct of the brigade in these terms:—"Major-General the Honourable Sir Charles Colville's brigade of the third division was seriously attacked in its advance by a very superior force, well formed, which it drove in, supported by Major-General Inglis's brigade of the seventh division, commanded by Colonel Grant, of the Eighty-second. These officers, and the troops under their command, distinguished themselves." In this battle, the battalion had Captain Adams, Lieutenant Higgins, Ensign Bolton, Volunteer Rees, and twenty-two rank and file, killed; with Captain Bateman, Lieutenants Galbraith, Welch, and Arthur Johnson, six serjeants and one hundred and twenty-seven rank and file, wounded. Lieutenant-Colonel Pratt obtained a medal, and by authority, dated October the 25th, 1817, the word "V<small>ITTORIA</small>" is borne upon the colours of the regiment.

After the battle of Vittoria, the F<small>IFTH</small> pursued the enemy in the direction of Pampeluna; if was subsequently sent against a French force under General Clausel, which however escaped to France. The battalion afterwards proceeded to Pampeluna, and was engaged towards the end of July near the village of Hörte del Reigen in front of that fortress. Having advanced along the gloomy passes of the lofty Pyrenean mountains, the regiment was stationed a short time at Olaque, in the pass of Roncesvalles, from whence it retired, on the advance of the enemy under Marshal Soult, to a position in the *Pyrenees*, in front of Pampeluna. Here the troops were attacked by the enemy, and after much hard fighting had occurred, the third division advanced across the heights in its front to turn the enemy's left flank, when the French were driven from their ground and pursued along the defiles in the mountains.

After passing through the Pyrenees the troops crossed the frontiers, and the interior of France resounded to the firm tread of the conquering British soldier. At the battle of *Nivelle*, on the 10th of November, the third division, under Major-General Colville (in the absence of Sir Thomas Picton), formed the right centre of the combined army, and advancing by the left of the village of Sarré carried the redoubts on the left of the enemy's centre, driving the French from their ground, and afterwards moving by the left of the river Nivelle upon St. Pé; in which affairs, the usual gallant conduct of the battalion earned a medal for its Lieutenant-Colonel Pratt, and permission by authority, dated October the 25th, 1817, for the word "NIVELLE" to be borne on the colours. In this battle, its loss consisted of one serjeant and fourteen rank and file, killed; Captain Clarke, Lieutenant Bird, three serjeants, and one hundred and nine rank and file, wounded; and Captain John Hamilton taken prisoner.

The regiment was afterwards employed in the operations connected with the passage of the river *Nive*; and was partially engaged in the action, on the 13th of December; after which it was cantoned in and about Hasparen, a town in the south of France, 13 miles from Bayonne.

1814

On the 14th of February, 1814, the battalion broke up from its cantonments, and on the 24th, it was sharply engaged with the enemy. Captain Culley, of the FIFTH, with the light companies of his own battalion, the Eighty-seventh, and Ninety-fourth, was ordered to force a deep ford of the river *Gave d'Oleron*; he effected the passage, but, being attacked by superior numbers, was driven back with considerable loss. Captain Culley, and Lieutenant R. Pennington, of the FIFTH, were severely wounded on this occasion, and the battalion lost seven rank and file, killed, and thirteen taken prisoners.

The battalion took part in the battle of *Orthes*, on the 27th of February; also in frequent and successful skirmishes with the French rear guard during its retreat through the vineyards between Pau, Vicq, and Tarbes, and finally, in the battle of *Toulouse*, the closing struggle and crowning victory of the Peninsular war, on which occasion the first battalion of the FIFTH behaved with its usual gallantry; its commanding officer, Colonel Pratt, received medals for the battles of Orthes and Toulouse, and by authority, dated July the 4th, 1818, the names of these battles are inscribed upon the colours. The loss of the battalion in the battle of Orthes was one Lieutenant, Hopkins, and eleven rank and file, killed; and thirty-three wounded: in subsequent actions it had one rank and file, killed, and twelve wounded.

The gallant exploits of the British troops having caused the overthrow of the tyrannical power of Buonaparte, hostilities ceased on the continent: the regiments went into quarters of refreshment, and the veterans of the FIFTH could now look back with exultation at the scenes of victory and triumph which had attended their career in this war. They could reflect with delight on the fame they had acquired, but especially at the glorious result, that their valour had preserved their native land from the presence of war, and their efforts had acquired peace for Europe.

On the extension of the most honourable military order of the Bath in 1815, Colonel Charles Pratt, of the FIFTH, was nominated a Knight-Commander, and Colonels the Honourable Henry King, and Edward Copson, Companions of the Order. The regiment also, in reward and commemoration of its services throughout the Peninsular war, received permission by authority, dated April the 22nd, 1815, to inscribe, in addition to its other distinctions, the word "PENINSULA" upon its colours.

Although peace had been restored to Europe, war was continued in America, and the first battalion of the FIFTH was allowed but a few days repose, before it was ordered to the scene of conflict. It marched out of quarters on the 11th of May, and arrived on the 20th at Bourdeaux, from whence, after a halt of eleven days, it embarked, and sailed for Canada, disembarking on the 7th of August at Sorel, on the river St. Lawrence, about one hundred miles above Quebec. From Sorel it marched to Chambly to join the troops encamped there under Lieutenant-General Sir George Prevost, and formed, with the Third, Twenty-seventh, and Twenty-eighth regiments, the brigade of Major-General Sir Manley Power. It was present at the unsuccessful attack made by Sir George Prevost on the Americans near *Plattsburg*, in the early part of September, and afterwards went into barracks at La Prairie; in November it marched to Montreal, detaching five companies to Coteau du Lac.

| 1815 |

Early in February, 1815, the first battalion moved from Montreal to Upper Canada, where three companies were stationed at Johnstown, and the remaining seven quartered at the farmers' houses along the St. Lawrence, and scattered over a space of nearly twenty-eight miles. But in May, these seven companies and head-quarters were re-assembled in Fort Wellington. Peace having been concluded with the Americans, early in June the battalion marched to Montreal, and sailing down the St. Lawrence in steam vessels to Quebec, it embarked on the 8th in four transports for Europe.

In the mean time the return of Buonaparte to France, in violation of the treaty of 1814, had rekindled the war on the continent, and the first battalion of the FIFTH was immediately ordered to France. After touching at Portsmouth, it disembarked on the 11th of July at Ostend; proceeded by the canal to Ghent, and marching from thence to Paris, joined the British troops encamped at St. Denis on the 24th of August, thus missing being present at the glorious and decisive victory of Waterloo, which, to a regiment, that had so conspicuously shared in all the peninsular campaigns, was at once a disappointment and a misfortune.

| 1816 |
| 1817 |
| 1818 |

Peace having again been concluded, an army of occupation was directed to remain in France for a few years; and in January, 1816, the first battalion of the FIFTH formed part of the garrison of the fortified city of Valenciennes; in July, August, and September it was encamped in the vicinity of that town, but returned to Valenciennes in October, and remained there till the month of April, 1817, when it went to Bapaume and the adjacent villages, and thence in July into camp at Cambray. In October it returned to Bapaume, and in June 1818, again joined the camp near Cambray, where the army was reviewed by the allied sovereigns. In October the first battalion of the FIFTH marched to Calais, and having embarked on the 31st for England, landed at Dover on the 1st of November, and marched for Winchester, where it arrived on the 10th of the same month.

In the mean time the second battalion, after recruiting to nearly its full numbers, in Exeter barracks, marched in November, 1813, to Chelmsford, and thence in the following month to Windsor, where it remained till October, 1815, when it was ordered to Gosport, and was there finally disbanded on the 24th of June, 1816.

| 1819 |

On the 4th of February, 1819, the regiment, now reduced to one battalion, embarked at Portsmouth for the West Indies; arrived on the 3rd of April in Carlisle bay, Barbadoes, and sailed again on the 5th (after being reviewed on the 4th by Lieutenant-General Lord Combermere) for the following destinations, *viz.*, five companies and head-quarters to Antigua, four to St. Christopher's, and one company to Montserrat.

On the 10th of July, 1819, Lieutenant-General Wynyard died, and on the 12th General Sir Henry Johnson, Bart., G.C.B., was appointed Colonel of the FIFTH.

| 1820 |
| 1821 |

The regiment occupied the stations before mentioned, until March, 1821, when five companies with head-quarters were ordered to St. Vincent's, three to Dominica, and two to St. Lucia. On the 25th of October this year, the establishment of the regiment was reduced from ten to eight companies.

| 1822 |
| 1823 |
| 1824 |

After remaining on the above station until January, 1824, two more companies with head-quarters were ordered to Dominica, and the remainder to St. Lucia.

The privilege which the corps for a long series of years enjoyed, of wearing a distinguishing feather, was this year confirmed to it by a letter from the Adjutant-General of the army, of which the following is a copy.

"Horse-Guards, 2nd July, 1824.

"Sir,

"I have had the honour to receive and submit to the Commander-in-Chief, your letter of 28th ultimo, and enclosure, and in reply am directed to signify to you, that under the circumstances therein stated, His Royal Highness has been pleased to approve of the *White Feather*, which for a long series of years has been worn as a mark of distinction by the FIFTH Regiment of Foot, being continued to be used by that corps.

"I have, &c.

(Signed)   "H. TORRENS, Adj.-Gen.

"Colonel Sir C. PRATT, K.C.B.,
    "5th Foot."

| 1825 |

On the 25th March, 1825, the regiment was augmented from eight to ten companies.

In May, 1825, Colonels the Honourable Henry King, C.B., and Sir Charles Pratt, K.C.B., who during the Peninsular war had led the corps in so many days of glory and of victory, were promoted to the rank of Major-Generals in the army: Sir Charles Pratt had been at the head of one or other of the battalions since 1808, and was succeeded in the command of the regiment by

63

Lieutenant-Colonel William Sutherland, from the second West-India Regiment.

1826

On the 16th of March, 1826, the head-quarters embarked at Dominica for England. The regiment landed at Portsmouth on the 12th and 22nd of April and 3rd of June, according as the transports arrived: marched in three divisions on the 22nd, 23rd, and 24th of June, from Cumberland Fort, and arrived on the 29th, 30th, and 31st, at Weedon, in Northamptonshire, where it was joined on the 24th of July by the depôt, consisting of four captains, four subalterns, one surgeon, one serjeant, and sixty-nine rank and file, from Tynemouth Castle. The corps remained at Weedon during the remainder of the year, and was joined during its stay in Northamptonshire, by one hundred and fifty-six recruits from its different recruiting parties.

1827

The FIFTH regiment marched from Weedon barracks in three divisions, on the 1st, 3rd, and 4th of January 1827, by route, to Hull, in Yorkshire, where it arrived on the 10th, 12th, and 13th of the same month, detaching one company to Bradford, one to Halifax, and on the 27th, one company to Brigg. At Hull one hundred and twenty-four men joined as recruits.

On the 28th and 29th of March, and 4th of April the regiment marched from Hull and the detached stations, and arrived on the 5th of April at Bolton, in Lancashire, having one field-officer and three companies detached at Blackburn, one company at Haslington, and one company at Accrington. During its stay at Bolton, the regiment received seventy-seven recruits from its parties, &c., and arrived at its full establishment, having recruited nearly five hundred men during the eleven months which had elapsed since its return from the West Indies.

1828

On the 10th and 17th of September, the regiment marched from Bolton, on route to Liverpool, and on the 19th and 20th the detached companies marched into Liverpool, in which town the regiment remained in billets until the morning of the 25th, when it embarked on board the "Britannia" and the "Birmingham" steam vessels for Ireland, and landed on the 26th at Dublin, where it was quartered in Richmond barracks. On the 15th of October it moved from the Richmond to the Royal barracks, and there remained until it was ordered to Athlone, for which station it marched on the 5th, 7th, and 17th of May, 1828, detaching one company to Shannon Bridge, from which a subaltern and twenty-five men were sent to Tullamore, one company to Ballymahon, (sending small parties to Ballinacarrig and Abbeyshrule,) and one company to Roscommon, having a subaltern and thirty rank and file at Strokestown. The detachment at Tullamore was ordered to head-quarters on the 6th of July.

A party of one hundred men under Major Tovey, marched from Athlone on the 6th of October to Shannon Bridge, and remained there during the fair at Ballinasloe. The detachment at Strokestown joined head-quarters on the 18th of October, and was again sent out on the 26th of January, 1829. On the 22nd of the same month, the company at Ballymahon was withdrawn, and joined the head-quarters at Athlone.

The colours of the regiment having been worn out in the course of its long and honourable service, a new set, after being solemnly consecrated in St. Peter's Church at Athlone, was presented on parade with the usual ceremonies, and a suitable address by Major-General Sir Thomas Arbuthnot, K.C.B., commanding the Connaught district. The General was pleased on this occasion to speak in the most flattering terms of the distinguished gallantry of the regiment in the field, and its good and orderly conduct in quarters.

The regiment marched to Castlebar, in the county of Mayo, on the 30th and 31st of March, 2nd, 3rd, 7th, and 9th of April, detaching two companies to Westport, under a field-officer; one company to Foxford, sending a subaltern and eighteen rank and file to Ballaghadareen, and one company to Dunmore. On the 2nd of May, two companies proceeded, per route, to Ballinrobe.

The distinction of wearing a white or grenadier feather, which the FIFTH regiment had proudly won for itself, having become extinct by the regulations of the 10th of February of this year (1829), which directed a white feather to be worn by the whole of the infantry of the army, rifle regiments and light infantry excepted, the commanding officer (Lieutenant-Colonel Sutherland) lost no time in applying, through General Sir Henry Johnson, Bart., G.C.B., the Colonel of the regiment, for an equivalent; this was graciously conceded by his Majesty, George the Fourth, and the distinction of wearing a feather different from the rest of the army, was continued to the corps in the following handsome terms in a letter from Lieutenant-General Sir Herbert Taylor, G.C.H., Adjutant-General of the Forces.

"Horse Guards, July 11, 1829.

"Sir,

"I have had the honour to receive and lay before the General Commanding-in-Chief your letter of the 6th of May last, with its enclosures, representing the anxiety felt by the officers and men of the FIFTH regiment, of which you are Colonel, to be allowed some distinction, as an equivalent for that which the regiment has lost in consequence of the regulations of the 10th of February last, prescribing a white feather to be worn by the whole of the infantry of the army, rifle regiments and light infantry excepted.

"On this occasion, Lord Hill commands me to say, that his Lordship enters fully into the feelings of the FIFTH regiment, and adverting to the gallantry of the exploits which obtained for that corps its original distinction, his Lordship has been pleased to submit to His Majesty, that the FIFTH regiment shall, in future, wear a feather half red and half white, the red uppermost, instead of the plain white feather worn by the rest of the army, as a peculiar mark of honour, whereby its former services will still be commemorated, and a perpetual incitement be afforded to a continuance of its good conduct.

"I have, &c.

(Signed)   "H. TAYLOR, Adj.-Gen.

"General Sir H. Johnson, Bart., G.C.B.
    "&c. &c."

1830

From Castlebar, Westport, and Foxford, the regiment marched on the 10th and 11th of September, agreeably to routes received, for Galway. Two companies, under a field-officer, were stationed at Oughterard; one company at Tuam, one at Ballinasloe, detaching one subaltern, one serjeant, and twenty rank and file to Mount Shannon, and a similar party to Kinavara. The company at Dunmore did not move on this change of the quarters of the regiment. On the 17th of November, the detachment at Kinavara joined the company at Ballinasloe, and on the 5th of April, 1830, one company from Oughterard proceeded to Banagher.

In August, 1830, whilst the regiment was stationed in Galway, a general election took place, and the representation of both the town and county was keenly contested; during the fortnight the elections lasted, the corps was constantly under arms and patrolling, and performed the harassing duty of that period with so much temper, conduct, and forbearance, that a public meeting was held, composed of the most respectable inhabitants of the town and its vicinity, including the several candidates and their supporters, and the following resolution, declaratory of their grateful sense of the good conduct of the regiment unanimously passed:—

"RESOLVED,

"That having witnessed the prompt, active, and efficient exertions of Lieutenant-Colonel Sutherland, the officers, non-commissioned officers, and privates of the FIFTH REGIMENT, in preserving peace and good order during the late contested election for the representation of this town, we deem it an act of justice thus to put upon public record the high value we entertain of their services; and that our worthy chairman is requested to convey to the gallant Commander of our garrison this expression of our warmest gratitude and thanks, and we request he will convey these sentiments to the officers, non-commissioned officers, and privates of the corps."

It may not be irrelevant to mention, that the FIFTH REGIMENT has always been remarkable for the good feeling that has subisted between it and the inhabitants of the different stations at which it has been quartered.

The regiment being ordered to Cork, the head-quarters and detachments marched from their respective stations on the 19th, 20th, 21st, 22nd and 23rd of October, and on the 26th it was countermanded to Buttevant barracks, where the several divisions arrived on the 27th, 28th, and 29th of the same month.

1831

A detachment was furnished by the corps to Mitchelstown on the 14th of February, 1831, and being removed on the 2nd of May to Galbally, it rejoined at Buttevant on the 15th of June.

On the 14th of March, the head-quarters, with four companies,—and on the 16th, four more companies, marched per route to Clare Castle, where they arrived to preserve order during the Clare election on the 17th and 19th, detaching one company to Kilrush, one to Corrofin, and subalterns' parties to Kildysart, Quinn, Kilkeshan, and Six Mile Bridge. The head-quarters marched to Ennis on the 30th of March; and the detachments at Quinn, Kilkeshan, and Six Mile Bridge, to the same place on the 6th of April. On the 5th of May the head-quarters returned to Buttevant, leaving eight companies detached in various directions (some being afterwards encamped) in the county of Clare, which was then, and had for some months been, in a very disturbed state—in fact, bordering on open rebellion. A small party of fifteen, half military (of the FIFTH) and half police, who were almost unarmed, having only a pistol and five rounds of ammunition each (being employed on a particular service), were attacked on the morning of the 8th of May, by some hundreds of the turbulent peasantry of the parish of Clondegad, in the county of Clare, and, in the course of a running fight, which was bravely sustained by these few men for several miles, Colour-Serjeant James Robinson of the grenadier company, was basely and barbarously murdered. His remains were buried at Ennis, and a handsome tomb with an appropriate inscription, placed over them by the regiment.

While the counties of Clare and Galway were in this disturbed state many of the magistrates declined to act. Under these circumstances, Lieutenant-Colonel Tovey and Captains McDonald and Spence, of the FIFTH regiment, were selected as gentlemen in whose firmness, prudence, and discretion, the Government could confide, and they received Commissions of the Peace for the above counties. The judicious conduct of those gentlemen as magistrates reflected credit on the regiment; their exertions were followed by happy results;—the two counties became tranquil, and the inhabitants returned to their peaceful and industrious habits[44].

On the 20th of September these companies were all concentrated at Buttevant; and a letter conveying the high sense entertained by Major-General Sir Thomas Arbuthnot of the good conduct of the regiment, of which the following is a copy, was received with the notification of their march from Clare:—

"Ennis, September 6th, 1831.

"Sir,

"In transmitting you the annexed notification of the arrival at Buttevant of several of your detachments from Clare, I am directed by Major-General Sir Thomas Arbuthnot to express to you the very great pleasure he feels in having to assure you, that both the officers and men of the FIFTH REGIMENT performed their duty, under most trying circumstances, during the disturbances in this county, to his perfect satisfaction in every respect.

"I have, &c.
(Signed)   "W. VINCENT, Lt.-Col., A.Q.M.G.

"Lieutenant-Colonel Sutherland,
        "Commanding FIFTH FOOT."

On the 16th of September, orders were received at Buttevant to hold the six service companies in readiness to embark for Gibraltar, and in consequence, the reserve, or depôt, was with great promptitude formed on the same day. On the 23rd the regiment was reviewed by Lieutenant-General Sir Hussey Vivian, K.C.B., Commander of the Forces in Ireland; and on the 29th it was inspected by Major-General Sir George Bingham, K.C.B., commanding the district, when both these distinguished officers expressed their unqualified approbation of its appearance, movements, and interior economy.

| 1832 |

The reserve marched on the 7th of November to Fermoy, being destined to remain for the present in Ireland, which continued in a very disturbed state; and the service companies moved to Cork towards the end of the month, and there embarked under the command of Lieutenant-Colonel Sutherland, on the

29th of November and 5th and 6th of December, on board the "Marquis of Huntley," (head-quarters,) "William Harris," and "Sylvia," transports; sailed from Cove on the 26th of December, arrived in the bay of Gibraltar, after a very quick but boisterous passage, on the 2nd, 3rd, and 5th, and disembarked on the 9th, 10th, and 12th of January, 1832, to do duty in that far-famed fortress.

Previous to the embarkation of the FIFTH from Ireland, the circumstance of the regiment having an "Order of Merit," a privilege established in this regiment in the year 1767 (as explained in page 37), attracted the attention, and elicited the representations, of the local military authorities. The commanding officer, after the arrival at Gibraltar, was in consequence called upon by the General Commanding-in-Chief, Lord Hill, to explain under what regulations and arrangements the Order was conferred, candidates selected, medals provided and distributed, and other particulars connected with this most laudable institution. The required information was promptly afforded, proved satisfactory, and the following gratifying letter was the result, viz.:—

"Horse-Guards, 20th June, 1832.

"Sir,

"I have had the honour to submit to the General Commanding-in-Chief, your letter of the 4th instant, with its enclosure, on the subject of the 'Order of Merit' existing in the FIFTH FOOT, and am directed to acquaint you, that the explanation afforded by Lieutenant-Colonel Sutherland, shows that the order in question is dispensed under the most laudable regulations, and has been productive of the best effects, during the long period since its original establishment in the regiment.

"It is considered highly desirable, however, that both officer and soldier should, under all circumstances, be taught to expect professional honours from the sovereign alone; and under this impression, Lord Hill has been induced to recommend to the king to give the royal authority for the confirmation and continuance of this regimental Badge of distinction, an arrangement, which, while it bestows upon it legitimate existence, will, at the same time, no doubt, enhance its value in the estimation of those on whom it is conferred.

"You will, therefore, be pleased to communicate this decision to Lieutenant-Colonel Sutherland, and acquaint him, that he is at liberty to proceed in the distribution of the medals and badges as heretofore.

"I have, &c.

(Signed)   "JOHN MACDONALD,

"Adjutant-General.

"Lieutenant-General
  "Sir William Houstoun, G.C.B., and G.C.H.,
    &c. &c. &c.,
  "Commanding at Gibraltar."

The "Order of Merit," which has been so long held by the regiment, consecrated and enhanced by purity and justice of distribution, and the real worth of the meritorious though humble individuals who earn so honourable a mark of good conduct, and brightened by the numerous distinguished services of the FIFTH REGIMENT since its foundation, is thus confirmed by the sanction of the Sovereign, the legitimate fount of honour, distinction, and reward.

1833

On the 27th of July, in this year (1832), the reserve companies of the regiment marched from Fermoy to Kilmallock, and in August to Bruff, where they continued until the 24th of January, 1833, when they proceeded to Nenagh: and from thence, in October to Templemore.

On the night of the 24th of April, 1833, whilst at Gibraltar, the roof of the Line Wall House, in which were the mess-rooms and the quarters of Lieutenant-Colonel Sutherland, suddenly burst out into an immense blaze of fire, in consequence of one of the wooden wall-plates, which had been carelessly built into the flue of a chimney, imperceptibly igniting the joists, lathing, couples, and lining of the roof over the ceiling: from the quantity of timber used in its construction, the house burnt with such fierceness and rapidity, that the ceilings of the rooms, almost instantly falling in, it was found impossible, notwithstanding the utmost exertions of the garrison, to save even the colours of the regiment, which were thus unfortunately, although accidentally, consumed.

1834

In June and July, 1834, that scourge, the cholera, attacked the garrison with such violence that the FIFTH lost one officer, two serjeants, one drummer, forty-one privates, three women, and four children, in all fifty-two souls, some of the former being among the finest and best-conducted young men in the regiment, whilst it may be mentioned, as a somewhat singular fact, that during the whole period of its ravages, not one case of cholera occurred in the Provost prison, at that time crowded with the most dissipated characters of the garrison, although it raged in the Artillery barracks, and the civil habitations in its immediate vicinity—an undeniable proof of the efficacy of abstemiousness and temperance, even though forced, on such occasions.

In the autumn of this year, the regiment having received orders to be prepared for removal to Malta, on the eve of embarkation the Lieutenant-Governor, Sir William Houstoun, G.C.B. and G.C.H., expressed his approbation of its conduct whilst under his command, in the following flattering terms:—

"Head-Quarters, Gibraltar,
14th October, 1834.

GARRISON ORDERS.

No. 1. "His Excellency, the Lieutenant-General Commanding, cannot suffer the FIFTH REGIMENT to embark from hence, without expressing his approval of the general conduct of this corps, during the period it has been under his command in this garrison, and he desires to offer his thanks to the officers, non-commissioned officers, and privates of this regiment, and more particularly, he begs to acknowledge his sense of the zealous and constant exertions of Lieutenant-Colonel Sutherland, which have so essentially contributed to maintain the discipline and good order of the corps under his command."

The regiment embarked in His Majesty's troop ship, "Romney," on the 15th October,—sailed on the next day,—and anchored on the 26th, after a very stormy passage, in the harbour of Valetta, under those stupendous fortifications which had been rendered famous by the prowess of the Knights of St. John of Jerusalem, and had for some generations been designated by the proud title of "the Bulwarks of Christendom:"—it disembarked without any accident or casualty on the 27th of the same month,—and for a short time occupied Fort Manoel.

The colour of the regimental facings was this year authorized by the subjoined letter to be changed to a handsome and lively green, viz.:—

"Horse-Guards, 30th June, 1834.

"Sir,

"With reference to the correspondence that has taken place respecting the Colour of the Facing of the FIFTH REGIMENT OF FOOT, of which you are Colonel, I have now the honour to acquaint you, that the Colour of the pattern exhibited by Lieutenant-Colonel Sutherland, with your sanction, has been approved by the King, and the General Commanding-in-Chief desires that the clothing of the regiment for the ensuing year may therefore be prepared accordingly.

"I have, &c.

(Signed) "JOHN MACDONALD,

"Adjutant-General.

"General Sir Henry Johnson, Bt., and G.C.B.
"Colonel of the FIFTH FOOT."

In September of this year (1834) the reserve companies marched from Templemore to Cork, where they remained ten months.

| 1835 |

General Sir Henry Johnson, Bart., G.C.B., having died on the 18th of March, 1835, at a very advanced age, was succeeded in the Colonelcy of the regiment, on the 25th of the same month, by Lieutenant-General the Honourable Sir Charles Colville, G.C.B. and G.C.H., who with much distinction, and especially in the affair at El Bodon, commanded the brigade in which the FIFTH served during a considerable period of the Peninsular war.

New colours having been received early this year to replace those accidentally consumed with the Line Wall House at Gibraltar, as before narrated, Major-General Sir Frederick Ponsonby, K.C.B., the Lieutenant-Governor, was requested to present them, but, a question having arisen relative to an additional banner[45] which the regiment had long carried, the subject was, after some discussion and correspondence, submitted to the decision of His Majesty, whose commands and pleasure on this head will be found in the following letter:—

"Horse-Guards, 31st July, 1835.

"Sir,

"I have the honour to acknowledge the receipt of your letter, dated 4th April last, which I have laid before the General Commanding-in-Chief, and by his Lordship's command the same has been submitted to the King.

"In reply to which, I am directed to acquaint you, that His Majesty considers it quite contrary to the established regulations, for any regiment to bear a *third Colour*, and on that ground he cannot consent to a flag or banner, which is stated to have been borne by the FIFTH REGIMENT since the year 1762, and which was accidentally destroyed by a fire at Gibraltar on the 24th of April, 1833, being replaced.

"His Lordship has received the King's commands to direct it to be made known to the officers and men of the FIFTH REGIMENT, that His Majesty has the strongest reason to be satisfied with the general conduct of the regiment, and, although His Majesty feels that he cannot comply with the request made on this occasion, by authorizing the additional flag, or banner, being retained by the corps, which, it must be stated, has never been sanctioned either by the Royal warrant of the 19th of December, 1768, or by any subsequent grant, yet his Majesty is desirous of conferring a mark of distinction on the regiment, which shall tend to perpetuate the record of its services at *Wilhelmsthal* in June, 1762: with this view his Majesty has commanded, that the regiment shall be distinguished by

72

wearing grenadier caps, with the King's Cipher, *W. R.* IV., in the front, and the ancient badge of the regiment, *viz. St. George killing the Dragon*, on the back part.

"I have, &c.

(Signed)   "John Macdonald,

"Adjutant-General.

"Lieutenant-Colonel Sutherland,
     "Commanding the Fifth Regiment, Malta."

The reserve companies embarked from Cork on the 1st of August, 1835, and proceeded to Dover, where they passed the succeeding fifteen months, and in October, 1836, marched to Gosport.

FIFTH REGIMENT OF FOOT (NORTHUMBERLAND FUSILIERS), M DCCC XXXV.

1836

His Majesty King William IV. having been pleased, in 1836, to approve of the corps being equipped as Fusiliers, and designated the "FIFTH REGIMENT OF FOOT, OR NORTHUMBERLAND FUSILIERS;" commissioned the Ensigns as second Lieutenants accordingly, and gave his Royal permission that the word "WILHELMSTHAL," in commemoration of *the field* on which it originally took its grenadier caps from the enemy, should be borne on its colours and appointments, as will appear by the subjoined copies of letters.

"Horse-Guards, 4th of May, 1836.

"Sir,

"I have the honour to acquaint you, by direction of the General Commanding-in-Chief, that his Majesty has been graciously pleased to approve of the FIFTH OR NORTHUMBERLAND REGIMENT OF FOOT, being in future equipped as a Fusilier Regiment, and being styled the FIFTH REGIMENT OF FOOT, OR NORTHUMBERLAND FUSILIERS.

"I have, &c.

(Signed)   "JOHN MACDONALD,

"Adjutant-General.

"Officer commanding the Fifth Regiment of Foot,
    "or Northumberland Fusiliers."

"Horse-Guards, 14th of May, 1836.

"Sir,

"I have the honour to acquaint you, by direction of the General Commanding-in-Chief, that his Majesty has been graciously pleased to permit the FIFTH REGIMENT OF FOOT, OR NORTHUMBERLAND FUSILIERS, to bear on its colours and appointments, in addition to any other badges or devices which may have heretofore been authorized, the word 'WILHELMSTHAL,' in commemoration of the gallantry displayed by the regiment while serving with the allied army, under Prince Ferdinand of Brunswick, at the battle of Groebenstein, on the 24th of June, 1762, particularly in the capture of a great number of prisoners belonging to the grenadiers of France, and the regiment d'Aquitaine, in the woods of 'WILHELMSTHAL.'

"I have, &c.

(Signed)   "JOHN MACDONALD,

"Adjutant-General.

"Officer commanding Fifth Foot,
    "or Northumberland Fusiliers,
        "Malta."

On the 14th of December, 1836, the Governor of Malta, Major-General Sir Henry Bouverie, presented the new colours to the regiment, drawn up for the purpose in review order on the Florian Parade.

His Excellency, on arriving in front of the line, was received with a general salute, the band playing and drums beating, after which the company on the right flank closed ranks, and was marched by its Captain in quick time (the band playing the grenadier's march) to the point in the front of the line, where the new colours were stationed, under a guard, and an escort of colour-serjeants; on arriving at which the company was halted, its ranks opened, and the colours, which appeared for the first time displayed, were saluted with

75

presented arms, the music playing "God save the King."

The march was then resumed in open order, and the colours escorted in slow time towards the left flank of the line, and thence to their appointed station in front of the centre, whilst the band and escort filed through the ranks to their posts on the right; the colours were received by a general salute from the regiment; arms were then shouldered, three sides of a square, open to the front, formed, and the service of consecration read in a most appropriate and impressive manner by the Rev. J. T. H. Le Mesurier, Chaplain to the Forces; the children of both sexes of the soldiers of the regiment, attired in uniform suits of new clothes that had lately been presented to them, repeating the responses.

Prayers being ended, His Excellency Sir Henry Bouverie handed the colours to the Lieutenants, under a general salute from the square, and then addressed the regiment in nearly the following terms:—

"Officers and Soldiers of the FIFTH Fusiliers,

"I am happy that it has fallen to my lot to present to you these colours. I do it in the full confidence that they will never be disgraced by insubordination, by loss of discipline, or misconduct in garrison, or in the field.

"The glorious deeds which are recorded in your annals, and inscribed upon these colours, will serve to incite in you the determination to equal them; to surpass them I believe to be impossible.

"The inspection, which I shall this day finish, of your regiment, will, I have no doubt, furnish me with the opportunity of reporting my entire satisfaction with the interior economy and management of the regiment, as well as with your movements in the field; and I trust that I shall never have occasion to alter the high opinion I have formed of you, not only here, but in scenes on service, of which I was myself a witness."

His Excellency having concluded his appropriate address, Lieutenant-Colonel Sutherland replied to the following purport.

"Permit me, Sir, on behalf of myself and the regiment, to return our best thanks for the very kind and flattering terms in which you have been pleased to present these colours. It must be a great additional source of gratification to all ranks to receive so honourable a charge from the hand of a distinguished officer, who, having personally witnessed the regiment in conflict with the enemy, can therefore duly appreciate its conduct; and this will doubtless prove a strong incitement to such a discharge of their duty, whenever they may have the good fortune to be similarly circumstanced, as will emulate those deeds to which your Excellency has so handsomely alluded."

The square was then reduced, and his Excellency having rode down the line, ranks were closed, open column formed, and the review commenced by marching past in slow and quick time, and in column at quarter distance. The manual and platoon exercises (the latter also kneeling as light infantry) were then performed, under the orders of Brevet Major Johnson, after which the Lieutenant-Colonel put the regiment through a variety of manœuvres and firings, in close, extended, and skirmishing order, of which his Excellency expressed his unqualified approbation.

In the evening his Excellency dined with the officers of the regiment at the mess, where a large party of about fifty persons, consisting of Vice-Admiral Sir Josias Rowley, the Captains of the squadron, commanding officers of corps, heads of departments, and staff, was assembled to meet him.

On the following Sunday the colours were, according to custom on such occasions, taken with the regiment to church; when the duties of soldiers, both as men and Christians, were inculcated by the chaplain to the forces in the most impressive manner.

| 1837 |

The regiment embarked from Malta on the 28th of March, 1837, and arrived on the 4th of April following at Corfu, where it has continued until the end of the year 1837, which brings this memoir to a conclusion.

The foregoing pages show that the FIFTH REGIMENT OF FOOT, OR NORTHUMBERLAND FUSILIERS, has preserved by its conduct in time of peace, untarnished, the laurels which it has acquired in war. Soon after its formation it availed itself of the opportunities which then occurred of acquiring a reputation for gallantry in action; and, under the influence of zealous officers and an excellent *esprit de corps*, it has conducted itself, in the various situations in which it has been placed during a period of more than one hundred and sixty years, so as to preserve its character and acquire additional honour. The distinctions which have, from time to time, been conferred on this corps, show the estimation in which its services are held:—the inscriptions which it bears on its colours are memorials of its gallantry in battles and sieges, where the British troops have acquired never-fading laurels, and have elevated the military character of their country, to the admiration of the nations of Europe.

∎

The Compiler of the Records of the Army feels it his duty to state, that Colonel Sutherland, of the FIFTH FOOT, OR NORTHUMBERLAND FUSILIERS, has evinced great zeal and devotedness in procuring information on all subjects in which the honour of his regiment is concerned, and furnished a statement of its services which has facilitated the preparation of this narrative for publication. The most effective assistance has also been afforded by Captain John Spence, of the same regiment, in the completion of this memoir.

∎

FIFTH REGIMENT OF FOOT (NORTHUMBERLAND FUSILIERS), M DCCC XXXVII.

[To face page 106.

FOOTNOTES:

[1] This treaty was conducted, on the part of Great Britain, by Sir William Temple, whose memoirs and correspondence on the subject are extant.

[2] "In this siege the Prince and the Rhingrave were ever at the head of the attacks, and made great use as well as proof, of the desperate courage of the English troops."—*Sir William Temple's Memoirs.*

"Amongst the rest of the troops that lay before the town, the English under Colonels Fenwick, Widdrington, and Ashley, to the number of 2600 men, petitioned his Highness to assign them a particular quarter, that they might be commanded separately, that so, if they behaved themselves like valiant men, they might have all the honour, and if otherwise, all the shame to themselves. This request his Highness readily granted, and they made it appear, by their fierce attacks, that they deserved this distinction."—*Boyer's Life of King William.*

[3] The English made their attack in the following order:—

2 Serjeants and 10 Firelocks.

1 Serjeant and 12 Grenadiers.

1 Officer, 1 Serjeant, and 12 Grenadiers.

1 Lieutenant, 2 Serjeants, and 30 Firelocks.

1 Serjeant and 12 men with Half-pikes.

1 Captain, 1 Lieutenant, 2 Serjeants, and 50 Firelocks.

1 Serjeant and 12 men with Half-pikes.

1 Captain, 1 Lieutenant, 1 Serjeant, and 28 men with spades and shovels.

   The support:

1 Captain, 1 Serjeant, and 58 Men.—*London Gazette.*

[4] "The English Brigade being frequently put on the most desperate attacks, and always behaving themselves according to their accustomed bravery; his Highness, after a very sharp night's service performed by them, gave each regiment a fat ox, and six sheep, which they killed and hung upon poles in sight of the army, to divide into equal parts to each company. Some of the Dutch murmuring at this bounty to the English in particular, were told that the same was given to save Dutchmen's lives, and therefore they ought to be thankful to his Highness for it."—*Life of Major John Bernardi.*

[5] "The Earl of Ossory with his troops performed wonders."—*London Gazette*, No. 1329.

Brussels.—"Many wounded men have been brought hither, which are most of the Prince of Orange's Guards, and the English and Scots regiments, who did things to the admiration of those that beheld them."—*London Gazette*, No. 1330.

"The Earl of Ossory, with the English and Scots regiments, engaged in the attack on the side of Castehau, in which the Officers and Soldiers, in imitation of his Lordship, who always charged with them, behaved themselves with that courage and bravery which is so natural to them, and consequently suffered much."—*Account of the Battle of St. Denis.*

[6]

"Whitehall, 4th July, 1685.

"This day three Scots Regiments of Foot, consisting of about 1500 men, lately come from Holland, marched through the city, on their way to Hounslow Heath, where they are to encamp. They are the best men, and best prepared for service, that ever were seen, having their tents, and all other necessaries of their own with them. To-morrow the three English Regiments are expected from Holland.

"I send your Grace the Articles of War, prepared by his Majesty's order for the present occasion.

"WILLIAM BLATHWAYTE,
"Secretary at War.

"To the Duke of Albemarle."

War-Office Records.

[7] While the Fifth was in England one of its officers, Cornet George Carleton, quitted the Dutch service, and obtained a commission in a newly-raised regiment on the English establishment. This officer served as a volunteer with the Fleet under the Duke of York in 1672 and 1673; and in the same capacity with the army, commanded by the Prince of Orange, from 1674 to 1676, when he obtained a commission in the Fifth. He saw much service in the reign of King William III.; and served during the war of the Spanish succession, as engineer, with the army in Valencia and Catalonia; and was made prisoner at the surrender of Denia in 1708. In 1728 he published an interesting narrative of his services, interspersed with many curious anecdotes, under the title of *Military Memoirs*, which are allowed to contain the best account extant of the services of the Earl of Peterborough in Spain. These memoirs were reprinted in 1741 with the title of *History of the two last Wars*, and again in 1743, with that of *Memoirs of Captain George Carleton*; and a new edition appeared in 1809, with the latter title.

[8] One of the officers who quitted the Dutch service on this occasion was Captain John Bernardi, of the Fifth. He obtained a commission in the regiment at its formation in 1674; had distinguished himself on several occasions, and had received many honourable wounds.

At the Revolution in 1688, he adhered to King James, and served in his cause in Ireland and Scotland. He subsequently resided in London, and being implicated in the plot to assassinate King William, in 1696, he was imprisoned. Although his guilt could not be established, and he was never brought to trial, yet he was detained in prison by authority of an Act of Parliament passed expressly for that purpose. After remaining upwards of thirty years in confinement, he wrote his life, which was published in 1729; and contains many interesting particulars relative to the early services of the regiment.

[9] *Life of Major John Bernardi.*—Rapin says only forty declared for King James.

[10] This officer's name is sometimes written Talmash.

[11] Boyer's Life of King William.

[12] Dalrymple.

[13] Boyer.

[14] Afterwards the celebrated General Wood, who was many years Colonel of the 4th Horse, now 3rd Dragoon Guards.

[15] London Gazette, No. 2661; Dublin Intelligencer; and Story's History of the Wars in Ireland.

[16] Inquiry into the Management of the War in Spain, Part II. Account of Embarkations, page 9. —*London Gazettes*, 4340, 4347, and 4348.

[17] "Estremos.—The enemy, having resolved to besiege Olivenza, or oblige the Portuguese to a battle, had all their heavy cannon and fascines in readiness before the town; but upon the approach of the four regiments lately arrived from Ireland, they retired in great precipitation, and sent away their cannon to Badajoz. These regiments are in very good condition, and will be able to do great service."—*Ibid.* No. 4350.

[18] In 1706, six hundred and sixty men of the Thirteenth Foot were formed into a regiment of Dragoons by the Earl of Peterborough, in Catalonia, and the Colonelcy conferred on the Lieutenant-Colonel, Edward Pearce. The remainder of the regiment returned to England to recruit, and, having completed the establishment, arrived in Portugal as above stated. The regiment of Dragoons thus formed was disbanded at the peace of Utrecht.

[19] Annals of Queen Anne, and London Gazette.

[20] The Monthly Mercury for May, 1709.

[21] London Gazette.

[22] Annals of Queen Anne, Vol. 10, page 95.

[23] London Gazette.

[24] The Marquis of Granby's Despatch.

[25] "The Brigade formed of the English Grenadiers and Scotch Highlanders greatly distinguished itself, performing wonders."—*Operations of the Allied Army*, page 161.

[26] "The FIFTH Foot behaved nobly, and took above twice its own numbers prisoners."—*Letter from an Officer of the Artillery.*

"Prince Ferdinand pursued and pressed upon them as close as possible: and they would, without doubt, have been entirely routed, if M. de Stainville had not thrown himself, with the Grenadiers of France, the Royal Grenadiers, the regiment of Aquitaine, and other corps, being the flower of the French infantry, into the woods of Wilhelmstahl to cover their retreat. That resolution cost him dear; his whole infantry having been taken, killed, or dispersed, after a very gallant defence, excepting two battalions which found means to get off; some of these troops had before surrendered to Lord Granby's corps, and upon the coming up of the army, the remainder, after one fire, surrendered to the FIFTH regiment of Foot."—*London Gazette.*

[27] Return of Prisoners taken in the action at Groebenstien, and in the woods of Wilhelmsthal, on the 24th June 1762.

CORPS.		Number of Men.
Grenadiers of France		635
Royal Grenadiers.	Rochelambert	208
"	L'Espinasse	135
"	Le Camus	121
"	Narbonne	60
Aquitaine		432
Poictou		29
Royal Deux-Ponts		30
Waldner		108
D'Epring		55
Choiseul,—Dragoons		64
Royal Picardy,—Cavalry		30
Fitz-James',—Cavalry		77
Chamboran		28
Monnet		112
Of different corps		446
		———
		2570
	Officers	162
		———
	Total	2732

Also one standard, six pair of colours, and two pieces of cannon, were taken.—*Operations of the Allied Army.*

[28] According to the embarkation return the strength of the regiment when it quitted Germany was, 27 officers, 692 men, 54 women, and 67 horses.

[29] A full account of these medals is given in a work published in America by General Donkin in 1777.

[30] How the badge of St. George and the Dragon with the motto "*Quo fata vocant*" above mentioned, were first acquired by the regiment, has not been ascertained. There is a tradition in the corps that they were conferred as an honorary distinction for gallant conduct either in the German war or that of the Spanish succession; but it is probable they might have been assumed when the regiment in 1675 was given to Colonel John Fenwick, and became English. A portrait of Major Bernardi (who was an Ensign in this corps at its formation in 1674, and rose to the rank of Captain in it) prefixed to his Memoirs published in 1729, is surmounted by the motto "*Quo fata trahunt*," evidently a metamorphosis of, and borrowed from the "*Quo fata vocant*" of the regiment. The Royal Warrants of the 1st of July, 1751, and 19th of December, 1768, while they recognise and confirm the badge, are silent respecting the motto; an omission, however, not confined to the FIFTH Regiment only, for the warrants do not notice the motto of any one infantry regiment, though others (the Royal Scots for instance,) must have had mottoes. It will be seen in the text that the motto surmounted the badge on the medal of merit, one of which from the original die with the date 10th of March, 1767, is now (1837) in possession of Colonel Sutherland, commanding the regiment. This motto and badge has for many years been borne on the officers' and men's appointments, and there is no doubt but they form one whole, and are coeval with each other.

[31] "Lord Percy now formed his detachment into a square, in which he enclosed Colonel Smith's party, who were so much exhausted with fatigue that they were obliged to lie down for rest on the ground, their tongues hanging out of their mouths like those of dogs after a chase."—*Stedman's History of the American War.*

[32] London Gazette.

[33] London Gazette.

[34] "If any thing had been wanting to show the bravery and discipline of the British troops, the action at Bunker's Hill furnished an ample proof of both. Twice they were stopped and twice they returned to the charge. In the middle of a hot summer's day; encumbered with three days' provisions, their knapsacks on their backs, which, together with cartouch-box, ammunition, and firelock, may be estimated at 125lbs; with a steep hill to ascend, covered with grass reaching to their knees, and intersected with walls and fences of various enclosures; and in the face of a hot and well-directed fire,—they gained a complete victory over three times their own numbers."—*Stedman.*

[35] Stedman.

[36] London Gazette.

[37] Lieutenant-Colonel Smith continued in the command of the fortress of Niagara until the 19th November, 1795, when he died, and was buried with military honours, in a vault prepared for the family on the Canada side of the Niagara River. His son, Sir David William Smith, baronet, was born in the regiment, and having obtained a commission at an early age, he attained the rank of Captain in it before he quitted the service; he afterwards settled in the province of Upper Canada, and was called to the bar there. He communicated to the compiler of this record, with great zeal and kindness, several interesting particulars relative to the history of the regiment. He died on the 19th of May, 1837, at Alnwick, in Northumberland.

[38] Now (1837) Lieutenant-General Sir Roger Hale Sheaffe, Bt.

[39] Marshal Soult, Duc de Dalmatia.

[40] Lieutenant-General Sir Arthur Wellesley, K.B., was created a Peer on the 26th August, 1809, by the titles of Baron Douro of Wellesley, and Viscount Wellington of Talavera.

[41] Late Scots Brigade, formed from the three Scots regiments, mentioned at page 10.

[42] "Ridge fell, and no man died that night with more glory:—yet many died, and there was much glory."—*Napier.*

[43] The chivalrous spirit displayed throughout these campaigns by private James Grant, of the second battalion, deserves to be recorded in these memoirs. This brave fellow was a native of Strathspey; being

a musician in the band, he was, as usual, left with it in the rear whenever there was any expectation that the battalion might be seriously engaged. On such occasions, however, Grant uniformly stole away from the band, appropriated to himself the arms of the first man he found in the field disabled from using them himself, and, being a tall, fine-looking soldier, fell in on the right of the grenadier company, and there fought till the day was won, when he returned to his instrument. In this manner he took part in the actions of Busaco, Sabugal, Fuentes D'Onor, El Bodon, and Salamanca, the storming of Ciudad Rodrigo, and was amongst the foremost in the escalade of the castle of Badajoz. From all these he escaped without a wound: he was appointed serjeant-major of the regiment in 1828; and he died in 1835 from the effects of a fall, at Malta, where a handsome tomb was erected by the regiment, on which his achievements were recorded.

[44] On the 21st May, 1831, Captain Spence (being a magistrate) was directed to proceed with his company to *Kilfenora*, by the following letter, viz.:—

"Ennis, 21st May, 1831.

"Sir,

"I am desired by Major-General Sir Thomas Arbuthnot to acquaint you, that as it is very desirable to have a magistrate stationed at *Kilfenora*, and as, moreover, he was extremely pleased with your zeal and exertions, while in command of a post, he has directed Lieutenant-Colonel Tovey to send your Company to Kilfenora, having every expectation that your services there will prove of much benefit to the country.

"I have, &c.

(Signed) "W. VINCENT, Lt.-Col., A.Q.M.G.

"To Captain Spence, FIFTH FOOT."

[45] The FIFTH regiment for many years carried a *small green silk banner*, inscribed with the badge, motto, number, and designation of the corps, at the head of the regiment, amidst the corps of band and drummers. This distinction is supposed to have originated from the battle of Wilhelmsthal, where the regiment took the colours of the French grenadiers—as stated at page 34.

SUCCESSION OF COLONELS

OF THE

FIFTH REGIMENT OF FOOT,

OR

NORTHUMBERLAND FUSILIERS.

.

DANIEL VISCOUNT OF CLARE,

Appointed in 1674.

Daniel O'Brien was one of the distinguished loyalists who attended King Charles II. during the period His Majesty was in exile on the continent, and he obtained at the Restoration the title of Viscount of Clare for his grandfather, who had frequently given proofs of his loyalty and attachment to his King, in the reign of Charles I. Daniel, the third Viscount of Clare, succeeded to the title in 1670, and having proceeded to Holland, after the treaty of London, in 1674, he obtained the Colonelcy of the FIFTH FOOT, then newly raised; but, being afterwards charged with holding a treasonable correspondence with the French, he relinquished his commission and returned to Ireland.

After the Revolution in 1688, the Viscount of Clare displayed great zeal in the cause of King James,—having raised two Irish regiments of foot and one of dragoons for the service of that unhappy monarch; he was also a member of the Privy Council in Ireland, and Lord-Lieutenant of the county of Clare. He served under King James at the battle of the Boyne, in 1690: and died in the same year.

JOHN FENWICK,

Appointed 2nd August, 1675.

John Fenwick was many years an officer of the Queen's troop (now Second Regiment) of Life Guards, in the reign of Charles II., and he served under the Duke of Monmouth in the campaigns of 1672 and 1673. In the succeeding year he obtained permission to proceed to Holland, and in 1675 he was appointed to the Colonelcy of the FIFTH FOOT, retaining, at the same time, his commission of Guidon and Major in the Life Guards.[46] After his recovery of a wound received during the siege of Maestricht, some angry expressions occurred between him and the Prince of Orange, when he quitted the Dutch service, returned to England, and resumed his duties in the Life Guards; and shortly afterwards he succeeded to the dignity of a Baronet.

In 1678 Sir John Fenwick was promoted to the rank of Brigadier-General, and appointed Colonel of a newly-raised regiment of foot, which was disbanded after the peace of Nimeguen. He was subsequently governor of Holy Island, one of the Inspecting-Generals of cavalry, and a member of Parliament for the county of Northumberland: and in 1687 he was promoted from the Lieutenant-Colonelcy of the Queen's troop of Life Guards, to the Colonelcy of the Fourth regiment of Horse, now Third Dragoon Guards, from which he was removed by the Prince of Orange at the Revolution in 1688. In 1695 he engaged in a conspiracy to raise an insurrection in behalf of King James, for which he was apprehended and brought to trial before the Parliament. No direct proof of his guilt could be produced, yet a bill of attainder for high treason was passed against him; and he was beheaded on Tower Hill on the 28th of January, 1697.

HENRY WISELY,

Appointed 1 th September, 1676.

Henry Wisely was an Officer of repute in the Dutch service, and his meritorious conduct was rewarded with the Lieutenant-Colonelcy of the FIFTH. After the resignation of Colonel (afterwards Sir John) Fenwick, he was promoted, at the recommendation of the Prince of Orange, to the Colonelcy of the regiment, by commission from the States-General of Holland dated the 11th of September, 1676. He served with his regiment against the French until the peace of Nimeguen, acquiring, by his zealous exertions on all occasions, the character of a good officer. He was drowned on his passage to England in the winter of 1680.

THOMAS MONK,

Appointed 10th December, 1680.

This Officer also served with distinction under the Prince of Orange, and was advanced to the Lieutenant-Colonelcy of Sir Henry Bellasis' regiment (now Sixth Foot), from which he was promoted to the Colonelcy of the FIFTH in December, 1680; but his death appears to have occurred before he acquired any higher rank.

THOMAS TOLLEMACHE,

Appointed 9th October, 1688.

Thomas Tollemache (or Talmash), son of Lionel third Earl of Dysart, was an officer in the English army in the reign of King Charles II., and in January, 1678, he obtained the rank of Captain in the Second Foot Guards. In March of the same year he was appointed Lieutenant-Colonel of Lord Arlington's newly-raised regiment, which was disbanded after the peace of Nimeguen. He was afterwards Lieutenant-Colonel of the First Foot Guards; but subsequently entering the Dutch service, he was promoted to the Colonelcy of the FIFTH in October, 1688; from which he was removed to the Colonelcy of the Second Foot Guards in May following. He was advanced to the rank of Major-General in December, 1690; and to that of Lieutenant-General in January, 1692. He commanded an expedition to the coast of France in the summer of 1694, was wounded at Cameret Bay on the 8th of June, and died on the 12th at Plymouth.

EDWARD LLOYD,

Appointed 1st May, 1689.

Edward Lloyd became proficient in the duties of his profession in active service under the Prince of Orange, who promoted him to the Colonelcy of the FIFTH FOOT in May, 1689. While serving with his regiment in Ireland, and in the Netherlands, he acquired the confidence and esteem of his superior officers, and he had every prospect of rising to high military rank; but his mortal career was terminated by death on the 26th of August, 1694.

THOMAS FAIRFAX,

Appointed 6th November, 1694.

This Officer, after a progressive service in the subordinate ranks, obtained, on the 8th of March, 1689, the Lieutenant-Colonelcy of Lord Castleton's regiment, from which he was promoted by King William III., in November, 1694, to the Colonelcy of the FIFTH FOOT. He served with his regiment in Flanders, was promoted to the rank of Brigadier-General in 1696, and commanded a brigade of infantry during the campaign of the following year. He was removed from the FIFTH in 1703, was afterwards promoted to the rank of Major-General; and died on the 6th of January, 1710.

THOMAS PEARCE,

Appointed 5th February, 1704.

Thomas Pearce obtained the commission of Ensign in a regiment of Foot on the 28th of February, 1689; and in October, 1694, he was appointed Captain of the Grenadier Company in the Second Foot Guards. He served at the siege of Namur in 1695, and, being engaged in storming the covered-way on the night of the 8th of July, he advanced, in the heat of the conflict, too far in front of his men, and was wounded and taken prisoner.

In 1702 he served under the Duke of Ormond in the expedition to Cadiz; and, commanding a brigade of Grenadiers at the storming of the forts of Vigo, he was wounded in the thigh by a cannon-ball. His gallantry was rewarded on the 10th of April in the following year with the Colonelcy of a newly-raised Irish regiment of Foot;[47] from which he was removed to the FIFTH, on the 5th of February, 1704. He was promoted on the 1st of January, 1707, to the rank of Brigadier-General, and, proceeding with his regiment to Portugal, he highly distinguished himself at the head of a brigade of infantry at the battle of Caya in 1709, and was taken prisoner. He was shortly afterwards exchanged for a French Brigadier-General, and on his return to England he was promoted to the rank of Major-General. He was further promoted to the rank of Lieutenant-General on the 5th of March, 1727; and in 1732 he was removed to the Colonelcy of the Fifth Horse, now Fourth Dragoon Guards. He was several years a member of Parliament for Melcomb Regis, and died in 1739.

JOHN COPE,

Appointed 15th December, 1732.

This Officer entered the army in the reign of Queen Anne, and was several years Lieutenant-Colonel of the Second troop of Horse Grenadier Guards. He obtained the rank of Colonel in the army on the 15th of November, 1711; and was promoted to the Colonelcy of the Thirty-ninth Foot on the 10th of November, 1730, from which he was removed to the FIFTH FOOT on the 15th of December, 1732. In 1735 he obtained the rank of Brigadier-General; in 1737 he was removed to the Ninth Dragoons; and on the 2nd of July, 1739, he was advanced to the rank of Major-General. He was several years on the staff of Ireland, and, after having been removed to the Colonelcy of the Seventh Dragoons in 1741, he proceeded in the summer of 1742 to Flanders with the army commanded by Field-Marshal the Earl of Stair. In the beginning of the following year he was promoted to the rank of Lieutenant-General; and, having signalized himself at the battle of Dettingen under the eye of his sovereign, he was constituted a Knight of the Bath.

In 1745 Sir John Cope was Commander-in-Chief in Scotland, and a small body of troops under his immediate command were defeated by the Highlanders under the Young Pretender at Preston Pans; which unfortunate circumstance enabled the rebels to penetrate into England and advance as far as Derby. He retained the Colonelcy of the Seventh Dragoons until his decease in 1760.

ALEXANDER IRWIN,

Appointed 27th June, 1737.

Alexander Irwin commenced his military career as Ensign on the 1st of October, 1689, and, after serving the crown nearly forty-eight years in various parts of Europe, he was promoted to the Colonelcy of the FIFTH FOOT, by commission dated 27th of June, 1737. He was promoted to the rank of Major-General on the 24th of February, 1744; he was subsequently on the Staff of Ireland, and also held the appointment of Lieutenant-Governor of Kinsale. He was further advanced to the rank of Lieutenant-General in 1748, and died four years afterwards.

CHARLES WHITEFORD,

Appointed 25th November, 1752.

Charles Whiteford entered the army as Cornet on the 3rd of May, 1720; and on the 27th of April, 1741, he was promoted to the Lieutenant-Colonelcy of the Fifth regiment of Marines, with which corps he served several years on the continent of America and in the West India islands. In 1752 King George II. conferred the Colonelcy of the FIFTH FOOT on Colonel Whiteford, who did not long enjoy the promotion; his decease having occurred in the summer of 1754.

LORD GEORGE BENTINCK,

Appointed 20th of August, 1754.

Lord George Bentinck, second son of Henry first Duke of Portland, received the appointment of Ensign on the 3rd of November, 1735; and having been promoted on the 12th of April, 1743, to the command of a company in the First Foot Guards with the rank of Lieutenant-Colonel, he served at the battle of Dettingen in June of the same year. He obtained the appointment of Aide-de-camp to the King on the 17th of March, 1752; and the Colonelcy of the FIFTH FOOT, in August, 1754. He was afterwards promoted to the rank of Major-General; and died at Bath on the 2nd of March, 1759.

STUDHOLME HODGSON,

Appointed 24th of October, 1759.

Studholme Hodgson, after serving several years in the army, was appointed, in 1745, Aide-de-camp to the Duke of Cumberland, whom he attended at the battles of Fontenoy and Culloden. He obtained the command of a company, with the rank of Lieutenant-Colonel, in the First Foot Guards, on the 22nd of February, 1747; and on the 30th of May, 1756, he was promoted to the Colonelcy of the Fiftieth Foot. He obtained the rank of Major-General on the 25th of June, 1759; and was removed to the Colonelcy of the FIFTH FOOT in October of the same year. In 1761 he was advanced to the rank of Lieutenant-General, and he commanded the land forces of a successful expedition against Belle-Isle in the same year, for which he obtained the approbation of the King, and was appointed, in 1765, Governor of Forts George and Augustus. In 1768 he was removed to the Fourth Foot; in 1778 he was promoted to the rank of General; and in 1782 he was removed to the Colonelcy of the Fourth Irish Horse, now Seventh Dragoon Guards. He was again removed, in 1789, to the Eleventh Light Dragoons, and on the 30th of July, 1796, he was promoted to the rank of Field-Marshal. He enjoyed this elevated rank two years, and died in the autumn of 1798, at the advanced age of ninety years.

HUGH EARL PERCY,

Appointed 7th November, 1768.

Earl Percy entered the army at an early age, and was first engaged in actual warfare under the Duke of Brunswick during the seven years' war in Germany. He obtained the rank of Captain and Lieutenant-Colonel in the First Foot Guards, on the 17th of April, 1762; and was promoted on the 7th of November, 1768, to the Colonelcy of the FIFTH FOOT, the command of which corps he retained nearly sixteen years, displaying, during that period, such distinguished military virtues, with a kind liberality, and a constancy of attention to, and interest in, the welfare and credit of the regiment, as endeared his name in the grateful remembrance of the officers and men. His Lordship commanded a brigade in America, and distinguished himself in the retreat from Lexington to Boston, and in the storming of Fort Washington near New York. In 1784 he was promoted to the Colonelcy of the Second troop of Horse Grenadier Guards; and succeeded, in 1786, to the dignity of DUKE OF NORTHUMBERLAND. In 1788 the Second troop of Horse Grenadier Guards was incorporated in the Second Regiment of Life Guards; and in 1806 his Grace was appointed to the Colonelcy of the Royal Regiment of Horse Guards, which he resigned in 1812. The decease of this respected nobleman occurred in 1817.

THE HONOURABLE EDWARD STOPFORD,

Appointed 1st November, 1784.

This Officer entered the army as Ensign in the Twenty-ninth regiment on the 16th of December, 1750, and, having attained the rank of Captain, he was promoted on the 17th of January, 1760, to the Majority of the Seventy-sixth regiment. On the 3rd of October, 1766, he obtained the Lieutenant-Colonelcy of the Sixty-sixth regiment, with which corps he served several years in Jamaica, and was promoted to the rank of Major-General in 1782. In 1784 King George III. conferred the Colonelcy of the FIFTH FOOT on Major-General Stopford, who retained this appointment until his decease in 1794.

SIR ALURED CLARKE, G.C.B.,

Appointed 25th October, 1794.

Alured Clarke entered the army on the 20th of March, 1755, as Ensign in the

Fiftieth regiment of Foot; he obtained the rank of Lieutenant in 1760; and his regiment proceeding to Germany in the same year, he served during the remainder of the seven years' war with the army commanded by Ferdinand Duke of Brunswick. On the 7th of January, 1767, he obtained the command of a company in the F<small>IFTH</small> F<small>OOT</small>. He was promoted to the Majority of the Fifty-fourth regiment in 1771; and to the Lieutenant-Colonelcy of the Seventh Fusiliers on the 10th of March, 1777. He served with his regiment in America, during the war with the United States; and was promoted to the rank of Colonel on the 16th of May, 1781. He was further advanced to the rank of Major-General on the 28th of April, 1790; and obtained the Colonelcy of the F<small>IFTH</small> F<small>OOT</small> in 1794. During the war of the French Revolution, when Holland had become subject to France, the British Government resolved to take the Dutch settlement at the Cape of Good Hope; and this place was captured, in the autumn of 1795, by a body of troops under Major-General Sir Alured Clarke, and a naval force commanded by Vice-Admiral Sir George Keith Elphinstone. The services of Major-General Clarke were afterwards transferred to the East Indies, in which country he held the local rank of Lieutenant-General from the 3rd of May, 1796; and he was promoted to the rank of Lieutenant-General in the army on the 26th of January, 1797. In 1801 he was removed to the Colonelcy of the Seventh Fusiliers; and in the following year promoted to the rank of General. He was subsequently advanced to the rank of Field-Marshal; and died on the 16th of September, 1832.

RICHARD ENGLAND,

Appointed 21st August, 1801.

Richard England entered the service in 1766, as an Ensign in the Forty-seventh Foot, in which regiment he attained the rank of Major on the 3rd of August, 1781, and was promoted to the Lieutenant-Colonelcy of the Twenty-fourth Foot on the 20th of February, 1783. In 1796 he was advanced to the rank of Major-General; in April, 1800, he was appointed Colonel-Commandant of the second battalion of the F<small>IFTH</small> F<small>OOT</small>, and in the following year he succeeded Sir Alured Clarke in the Colonelcy of the regiment. In August, 1803, he was appointed Governor of Plymouth; he obtained the rank of Lieutenant-General in September of the same year, and died on the 7th of November, 1812.

WILLIAM WYNYARD,

Appointed 27th November, 1812.

William Wynyard was appointed to a Lieutenancy in the Sixty-fourth Foot on the 12th of June, 1777: he was afterwards Captain in the Forty-first regiment;

and in April, 1795, he was appointed Captain and Lieutenant-Colonel in the Second Foot Guards. In 1802 he attained the rank of Colonel in the army, and was appointed Colonel of the Royal West India Rangers on the 25th of October, 1806. His commissions of General Officer were dated—Major-General, 25th October, 1809, and Lieutenant-General, 4th of June, 1814. He was appointed Deputy Adjutant-General to the Forces, on the 9th of January, 1799, which situation he held (much respected by his official brethren at the Horse-Guards) until June, 1814, when, having been promoted to the rank of Lieutenant-General, he was appointed to the command of the Yorkshire District. He retained the Colonelcy of the FIFTH FOOT, to which he was appointed in 1812, until his decease, on the 10th of July, 1819.

SIR HENRY JOHNSON, BART., G.C.B.,

Appointed 12th July, 1819.

After serving in the subordinate commissions, this officer was promoted to the Lieutenant-Colonelcy of the Seventeenth Foot on the 4th of October, 1778, and, serving with his regiment in America and the West Indies, he obtained the rank of Colonel in the army on the 25th of December, 1782. In 1793 he was promoted to the rank of Major-General; and he obtained the Colonelcy of the Eighty-first Foot on the 18th of June, 1798. He commanded a body of troops in Ireland during the rebellion of 1798, and obtained great credit for his conduct in an action at New Ross. In the succeeding year he was promoted to the rank of Lieutenant-General; and to that of General on the 25th of April, 1808. After the decease of Lieutenant-General Wynyard, the Colonelcy of the FIFTH FOOT was conferred on General Sir Henry Johnson: he was many years Governor of Ross Castle; and died in 1835.

THE HONOURABLE SIR CHARLES COLVILLE, G.C.B. and G.C.H.

Appointed 25th March, 1835.

FOOTNOTES:

[46] War-Office Records.

[47] This regiment was disbanded in 1711.

LONDON:

Printed by WILLIAM CLOWES and SONS,
14, Charing-Cross.